How to Hear Classical Music

RU

11

THE GINGER SERIES

how to hear classical music
davinia caddy

AWA PRESS

First edition published in 2013 by Awa Press,
Level 3, 11 Vivian Street, Wellington 6011, New Zealand.

Copyright © Davinia Caddy 2013

National Library of New Zealand Cataloguing-in-Publication Data
Caddy, Davinia, 1980-
How to hear classical music / Davinia Caddy.
(Ginger series ; 11)
Includes bibliographical references.
ISBN 978-1-8775510-0-0 (paperback)—ISBN 978-1-8775519-8-7 (epub)—
ISBN 978-1-8775519-9-4 (mobi)
1. Music appreciation. 2. Music—Philosophy and aesthetics.
I. Title. II. Series: Ginger series (Wellington, N.Z.) ; 11.
781.17—dc 23

Typesetting by Jill Livestre, Archetype
Printed by Midas Printing International Ltd, China
This book is typeset in Walbaum

Find more great books at awapress.com.

For Chris

ABOUT THE AUTHOR

DAVINIA CADDY is senior lecturer at the
School of Music, University of Auckland,
where she teaches the history, theory and
analysis of music. She began her musical
career playing principal flute in the UK's
National Youth Orchestra, gained a PhD
in music from Cambridge University, and
carried out post-doctoral research at Oxford.
Her book *The Ballets Russes and Beyond:
Music and Dance in Belle-Époque Paris* was
published by Cambridge University Press
in 2012.

*The arts are not just a nice thing
to have or to do if there is free
time or if one can afford it ...
they define who we are as people.*
MICHELLE OBAMA

Real estate

'THE HOUSE IS IMMACULATE. A beautifully maintained character villa, with polished floors, Victorian fireplace and three plus bedrooms, it has that desirable indoor–outdoor flow to a sunny and private garden. Quiet cul-de-sac location. Much to offer the entry-level buyer to this city-fringe suburb. Don't let this one slip away!'

For once, the real estate guff seems right. This house, the sixty-third we've seen in the past five months, is nice. Perhaps too nice. The agent points to the minimalist kitchen with all-new appliances, the bathroom with his and her sinks. There's even a spa pool outside, a TV on the fridge door, and a huge painting that looks like a Mark Rothko over the fireplace.

And what's in here? I turn into a small room at the side of the house. The walls are painted beige. There's a lounge chair in the corner, and an expensive-looking Persian rug on the floor, but something else catches my eye – a book on top of a shiny black upright piano. As I cross the room I make out the lettering on the front cover: 'Jules Massenet, *Esclarmonde*, 1889'. It's the orchestral score to a little known and long forgotten opera by the French composer. Flicking the yellowed corners and stretching the cloth-bound spine, I notice some pages have been stuck together, although the tape is peeling away in places. Other pages have been scribbled on, pencil circles scrawled around musical notes and directions. The first page bears what looks like the signature of the composer himself: *J. Massenet. Paris, Octobre, 1889.*

Crikey, what a find. Captivated by the treasure in my hands, I start to muse. First, the tape. Was it used by Massenet to bind together and so delete certain pages of the score? Is it evidence of a process of revision? As for the scribbles, they are easier to fathom: they indicate what to play up, play down, or just play correctly during a performance – they're like Post-it reminders. What about the heritage of the score? It's surely a first edition. I might have spent years in back-alley Parisian book-shops searching for something like this.

I rush out, clutching the score to my chest and nearly tripping over the Persian rug. I want to know where the score has come from, how long the owners have had it, and what it is doing in this house.

Hang on a moment. *What is it doing in this house?* I look back into the room and visualise the score in its spot on the piano. There are no other scores – no other objects – in sight.

I think for another moment. *How is this score to be played?* The owners would have a hard job dealing not only with the tape but with the sheer size of the volume. It barely fits on the stand. Then there's the nature of the score itself. An orchestral score comprising parts for 30 or so instruments, some of which play in different keys, some of which use different notational systems: this isn't easy to play on the piano. A pianist wanting to play through an opera would prefer a piano-vocal score, a reduction of the orchestral parts for two hands. An orchestral version like this is useful only for conductors wanting to produce the opera, or for music historians like me, eager to pore over relics from the past.

The moment of revelation coincides with a tap on the shoulder. (It's my partner, with news of a built-in barbecue.) This score of Massenet's isn't to be played. Holding pride of place in the beige room, it's to catch the eye, not the ear. More than this, it's there to signal something: Music, with a capital M.

In case you're interested, I didn't buy the house. (It sold for almost double its market value – so much for the recession.) And I didn't talk to the owners. (They were holidaying in Fiji.) But I did find out, via the agent, that no one in the family had played through the opera. No one even played the piano, apart from an ambidextrous two-year-old. The score had been handed down from a great-great-aunt, a singer who had studied in Paris in the early 1900s.

The score was now a piece of musical real estate. Like the fancy sinks and appliances, it served to impress. Perhaps the owners wanted to exude a scent of culture and sophistication, to signal to potential buyers, people like them, that with the house came a certain lifestyle. What better way than to dig out the hefty volume from Paris (Paris!), wipe off the dust, and place it – carefully, alone – on top of the piano? And the score sure looked good – old, enchanting and, best of all, complicated, unintelligible to all but the musically literate.

I started to wonder: has classical music come to signify the pretensions of the wealthy? Is it merely a bauble, a status symbol, a pretty decoration on a piano that no one plays? Or is it more than this, a fashion-forward art form for the twenty-first century?

Here's what I think.

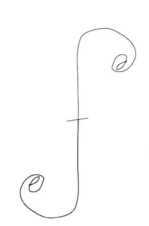

Without music, life would be a mistake.

FRIEDRICH NIETZSCHE

Play me,
I'm yours

I N THE MIDDLE OF a concrete concourse near the steps to London's Millennium Bridge, there's another piano. It looks odd, not only out of place but brightly painted and emblazoned with the words 'Play me, I'm yours'. It sounds odd too. Bought for a few hundred dollars, so I'm told, it makes a tinny tinkling noise, like something from a Western saloon. Yet it's drawing quite a crowd. Camera-clutching tourists and Londoners on their lunch breaks are happily milling around, taking in the sight – and the sounds – of George.

George – I don't catch his surname – is playing the piano. He can be only nine or ten, dressed more for football than a public performance. Still, he's captivating, his small hands swooping over the keyboard, his fingers fluttering like wings. He has that virtuoso look about him, where the performer appears transfixed, his or her body swaying back and forth, animated by a kind of musical electrical current. So it's fitting that George is tackling a virtuoso favourite, the third and final movement of Ludwig van Beethoven's Piano Sonata No. 14, commonly called the 'Moonlight'.

(Incidentally, the title was coined by a German music critic, Ludwig Rellstab, several years after Beethoven's death. It alludes to the sonata's first movement, which reminded Rellstab of the play of moonlight on the waters of Lake Lucerne in Switzerland. The term 'sonata' comes from the Latin *sonore* – to sound – and describes a three- or four-movement composition for a solo instrument.)

Sneak away from George, if you can, and walk over the Millennium Bridge. Does it shake? It used to: when it was first erected, Londoners nicknamed it the Wobbly Bridge. A few steps away, inside the courtyard garden of St Paul's Cathedral, you'll find another piano, just as old and honky-tonk, and just as brightly decorated.

A man in a suit walks up to this piano. Still standing, he plays a few notes and tries to string them together. It sounds a bit like the opening to Johann Pachelbel's famous Canon in D. But then the man scuttles off, apparently embarrassed.

Next, a young mother settles herself on the piano stool; her baby is sleeping soundly in one of those trendy three-wheeler prams. With regular glances at her child, the woman stumbles through 'Für Elise', although one of the F keys on the piano doesn't work. (This piece, also by Beethoven, was originally titled Bagatelle No. 25, bagatelle meaning 'trifle' and suggesting a frivolous, light-hearted piano composition. It was dedicated to a female friend and pupil of the composer, although whether this woman was actually called Elise is a mystery.)

Another man appears, younger, calmer and more confident than the first. It's Gwilym Simcock, the award-winning pianist and composer, recently voted one of London's most influential musicians. With a signature style that fuses classical music and jazz, Simcock is here to play for a performance by the Sydney Dance Company, which is about to take place in the courtyard.

Yes, here in the courtyard. You might call it a pop-up performance, a version of the much-hyped flash mob, where a group of people assemble in a particular place at a particular time and then, without warning, start to dance or perform some other activity to a crowd of unsuspecting onlookers.

There's a crowd gathering now, but they're far from unsuspecting. That's because Simcock and the Sydney dancers are regulars on the London scene. In recent weeks they've 'popped up' at several city hotspots, performing at Canary Wharf, Whitehall, Marble Arch, Victoria, Portobello Road, Soho and St Pancras railway station. (The station is a pop-up favourite. The BBC Symphony Orchestra – with the BBC Symphony Chorus and 150 amateur singers – performed Beethoven's 'Choral' Symphony here in November 2011.)

There are pianos in all these London locations: in fact, there are 50 pianos dotted around the city, carefully positioned near landmarks and beauty spots. And there are the same sort of pianos all over the world, not in homes, schools, studios, concert halls, churches, conservatoires and theatres – the usual musical venues. Walk the streets of Los Angeles, Salt Lake City, São Paulo, Geneva, Paris, Toronto or Toowoomba and you may be surprised what you find.

Luke Jerram is the man responsible for this growing piano population. A British artist known primarily for his sculptures and installations – so-called 'site-specific' modern art – Jerram has been providing the public with pianos since 2008, when his project 'Play me, I'm yours' launched in the UK.

The project has a social purpose. Disgruntled with the fast-paced, time-strapped modern-day society, Jerram wants people to slow down, pause for a moment and talk to one another – in his words, to 'take ownership of their urban environment'. The pianos were designed as a 'catalyst for conversation'. Scattered around cities and available at no expense, they would function like

Facebook or Twitter, as designated sites for social interaction. Gathered around them, complete strangers would share stories, memories, and seemingly useless information. They'd tell whoever would listen about Aunt Agnes who could have been the next best thing, the female Liberace, if only she hadn't married Uncle Seamus and bought a bakery with him in County Down…

Watch people playing or listening to or talking about these pianos – if there isn't one near you, check out the videos on YouTube – and you'll notice something else. Something obvious. Something tangible. Yet something that may surprise. We love classical music, love to make it (remember George), chance it ('Ür Elise'), and share it with those around us. We love to take ownership of it, you might say, borrowing Jerram's words.

Of course, we rarely say we do – at least we don't say it out loud and in earshot of others. And statistics (diminishing audiences and cuts in government funding) may tell a different story. Indeed, signs that classical music's in trouble are easy enough to find. It has all but vanished from schools, for example – although there is a school in England where the head teacher plays Handel and Verdi during lunchtime detentions, hoping the music will punish errant students and deter them from reoffending!

It's vanishing from mass media. Print newspapers (which may themselves be vanishing) are getting rid of classical music critics, and public radio stations, which have a long musical history, now prefer news, talkback and Top Ten pops.

So Jerram's project brings good cheer: smiles, laughter, stories and applause, or just moments of quiet reflection. All those pianos are heart-warming to see, and to hear. But not only because they remind us of days gone by – musicians we knew (or were), pieces we heard (or played), instruments we tried (and failed) to master. They remind us of our basic appetite for classical music, our attraction to its sonorous magic.

Let's remember, Jerram chose pianos. He could have set up chess games, taught t'ai chi, given away free coffee or soccer balls. All these would have fulfilled his original purpose of bringing people together and sparking conversation. But classical music offers something else, something above and beyond the opportunity for mere social networking.

Ask E.T.A. Hoffmann, a nineteenth-century German writer. 'Is not music,' Hoffmann once reflected, 'the mysterious language of a faraway spirit world whose wondrous accents, echoing within us, awaken us to a higher, more intensive life?'

Ask Michael Tilson Thomas, the conductor of the San Francisco Symphony Orchestra: 'What classical music does best, and must always do more, is to show a kind of transformation of moods, a very wide psychological voyage.'

Even the ancient Greeks acknowledged this emotional, intuitive aspect. Referring to the pipe and string instruments of the day, Aristotle described music's 'power of purifying the soul'. Plato, his teacher, put it more eloquently: 'Music gives a soul to the universe, wings to the mind, flight to the imagination and life to everything.'

Life to everything. Whether playing or listening, humming or whistling, or simply flailing your arms about pretending to conduct, music can make you feel alive, awed, raised to a new level of consciousness. Indeed, it never stops surprising me how a Beethoven sonata, a folk song by Aaron Copland, an opera by Dmitri Shostakovich — how all these pieces, so different in themselves, can trigger a creative impulse, change our perceptions, and make us feel a little different.

So what would you play if you stumbled across one of Jerram's pianos? And what would you like to hear? What would make you stop in your tracks during your rush about town, and take a moment to pause and listen?

I'd happily spend some time with Frédéric Chopin's *Études* or Claude Debussy's *Children's Corner*, both pieces for solo piano. Or I'd try to accost a singer and romp through Robert Schumann's *Dichterliebe*, a cycle of some of the most poignant love songs you'll ever hear. Any of these would make my day — and make for a refreshing change. As a music historian – a 'musicologist' in academic jargon – I spend hours thinking, talking, debating and writing about classical music, trying to convince other people, including some of my students, of its virtues. To some extent I'm lucky. I teach in a university where all sorts of music – not just classical, but pop, jazz, electronic, and even the new-fangled 'sonic arts' – are very much alive. Yet I sometimes struggle to reconcile the work I do with the music I hear. I forget to register the ground-level experience of classical music, what it's like to be seduced by a really good piece.

So I've learned a thing or two from Jerram's project. Certainly, all those pianists loom large over the pages of this book. Their have-a-go attitude and unabashed enthusiasm is catching, irresistible, a reminder of the pleasures and rough edges of musical experience. This is not to forget the project's 'street' appeal, how Jerram brings music to the masses, offering people of all ages, abilities and walks of life the chance to play, to observe and to listen. But what I really love about Jerram's idea – and what I'd like to celebrate in the pages that follow – is its sense of daring, its promise of change. Yes, Jerram tells us, you can listen to Beethoven's 'Moonlight' sonata live and en route to St Paul's. Yes, you can put a piano in the courtyard of a cathedral and watch a pop-up musical performance. And yes, you can even mix classical styles with jazz – à la Gwilym Simcock – while accompanying some of Australia's best dancers.

The doomsayers may tell you that classical music is (at worst) dead or (at best) dying, of little relevance today. But Jerram's project provides evidence to the contrary, evidence of the classical repertoire's continued hold over listeners, and of its ability to find a place in our fast and frenzied world.

The idea that classical music is the province of white-wigged old farts shows a failure of imagination, and rank snobbery.
STEPHEN FRY

Hooked on classics

I'M A CHILD OF THE '80s, the decade of shoulder pads, shell suits, leg-warmers and dungarees, big hair, Dire Straits and *Dallas*. As legend has it, we children whiled away our days with Care Bears, He-Man and She-Ra; our teenage siblings watched MTV; our grandmothers knitted square-end ties. As for our parents, when they weren't out forging careers they were sharing the housework, vacuuming, cleaning, cooking and ironing to the latest musical sensations. But no, not to Madonna, Whitney, Prince and Wham! According to *mumsnet.com*, an earnest social site 'for parents by parents', the soundtrack of choice for '80s stay-at-home mothers was *Hooked on Classics*, a compilation album produced by RCA Records under the K-tel label, with Louis Clark, former music arranger for the British rock group The Electric Light Orchestra.

Released in 1981, *Hooked on Classics* shot to fame, and its pop-infused classical style and up-tempo beat spawned a series of spin-offs: *Hooked on Mozart, Hooked on Romance, Hooked on a Song*. And knock-offs: *Hooked up Classics, Classical Muddley*.

I stumbled upon an old cassette tape a few weeks ago while clearing out a friend's stairwell. The gaudy cover caught my eye; it reminded me of the strip lights at a school disco I'd rather forget. But I hadn't forgotten the album, let alone the music on it. A techno-fuelled Toccata in D Minor. A disco version of the 'Hallelujah Chorus'. This was classical music for the Spandex generation, the motivational music of the decade.

It certainly motivated me. Slipping the cassette into an old machine lying among the stairwell junk, I started to shift from side to side and pump my fists in the air. No surprise, then, that I hurried through the cleaning, humming along to the recognisable melodies while swinging my arms and legs in time to the synthesised fast-paced beat.

The music that day didn't just get me moving. I also started to think about the classical repertoire and what the album could teach us about it. The term 'classical music' has the dubious honour of being both useful and useless. We know this sort of music when we hear it, of course. And we probably know where we will hear it, at what kind of occasion, and how we in the audience will be expected to react. Yet try to define it and we face an immediate challenge. What's in, what's out? What's classical, what's not?

Various definitions have been bandied about. Academics tend to point to a specific musical style, one associated with eighteenth-century ideals of clarity, grace and beauty. Others, writing for the general public, refer to a wider-ranging category embracing the gamut of instrumental, vocal, solo, ensemble, choral and operatic music. And then there are those who shy away from all stylistic references, gesturing instead to a (so-called) educated, (specifically) male and (exclusively) European musical tradition that developed over the centuries in line with trends in music's sister arts – painting, literature and theatre.

So what exactly is classical music? To what – and to whom – do the two words refer? And can *Hooked on Classics* offer any clues?

1 A ghostly presence

Let's take three composers from the album: Johann Sebastian Bach, Joseph Haydn and Giacomo Puccini. Bach's music dates from the early 1700s, a time when people threw their rubbish into the streets and cleaned their teeth with salt, if they cleaned them at all. Haydn probably had a toothbrush – he led a privileged life in the court of the Eszterházys, one of the wealthiest families in the Austrian Empire – but, as was customary in the eighteenth century, he relied for transport on four-legged friends. Puccini, on the other hand, had a car. In fact, he loved cars. But his eight-cylinder Lancia limousine, purchased in 1923, lacked the trappings and technology of the modern automobile.

Needless to say, all three composers are brown bread, buried long ago: Bach in the cemetery of the Johannes-kirche, Leipzig, where his grave went unmarked for over 100 years; Haydn in the Hundsturm cemetery, Vienna, although his remains were later moved to Eisenstadt, the seat of Eszterházy family; Puccini in Milan, a temporary resting-place until his body could be transferred to the family estate at Torre del Lago.

All the other composers on the album are dead too, and several have burial histories as convoluted as the above-mentioned three. Indeed, the bodies of many of the alleged Great Composers were buried, excavated and reinterred as scientists sought biological evidence – sometimes through dubious methods – of their creative genius.

According to *Hooked on Classics*, then, classical music is that of the dead. Which sounds about right: you'd be hard pushed to name a 'classical' composer alive today.

Sure, there are composers composing. John Adams, Thomas Adès, George Benjamin, George Crumb, Gareth Farr, Philip Glass, Robin Holloway, Lowell Liebermann, John Psathas, John Rutter, John Tavener, Judith Weir, Gillian Whitehead: these are just some of today's celebrated and successful crew. But you wouldn't call their music 'classical', would you?

2 Of long life and influence

Like old news, serious fun and boneless ribs, classical music is a contradiction in terms. The word 'classic' – think of classic cars, classic films, classic jokes, classic fiction – represents a gold standard. But it also invokes the past, telling us that something from years gone by still has quality, value and worth.

Classical music is no exception: the 'c' word confers long life and influence, respect and familiarity. According to *Hooked on Classics*, the music on the album is not just old but timeless, not just historical but hummable. And hum, back in the '80s, we did.

3 As poppy as pop

It's got a beat (a pulse, regular like a heartbeat), a metre (a pattern or hierarchy of beats), rhythm (a pattern of musical movement through time), melodies (tunes that stick in your mind), phrases (melodic constructions, a bit like sentences), and larger-scale structures (groups of phrases) that can recur throughout a piece. It's lively, catchy, invigorating, danceable, entertaining, easy on the ear and familiar. And it can function as ambient music, the background to some other more important activity.

In other words, classical music is not dissimilar to '80s pop. Indeed, with the simple addition of a fast-paced and percussive beat it can easily *become* '80s pop and be listened to in the same way – as a reverberating backdrop to your daily routine.

Or not. When *Hooked on Classics* was released, this insinuation caused a stir. The album spawned a new breed of listeners hooked on its high-energy tunes, but it also received a good deal of criticism, largely from the professional musical establishment and a raft of connoisseurs.

To these parties it was plain wrong – even sacrilegious – to equate classical music with pop. The former was serious and superior, 'art' music, 'unencumbered by the debris that drifts through the world of life', to quote one English critic. Based on complex underlying structures, classical music demanded our full and focused attention: we had to listen carefully, ears pricked and brain cells firing, to appreciate its true value and substance. Pop music, on the other hand, made no demands on our ears. It was simple, repetitive and crass, with a focus on surface effects rather than internal logic. It was not art but entertainment, and wholly dependent on the 'world of life', its people, societies and consumer trends.

From where I'm standing, this argument has a whiff of something rotten. But what do you think? Does classical music really make for a more 'artistic' experience? Is it actually superior to pop? Why can't the two types of music mix? And is there any evidence that they're incompatible? For answers, let's look over the life and times of perhaps the most famous classical icon of all.

Wolfgang Amadeus Mozart, born to Leopold and Anna Maria in Salzburg in 1756, was a jobbing composer, a 'working stiff', to quote American scholar Neal Zaslaw. And this stiff rarely lifted a finger without a formal commission – a request for an opera, a symphony, or a piece to celebrate a social event. Mozart certainly took pride in his music and his own compositional development, but he wasn't driven to compose by divine inspiration or some kind of psychological muse. He composed in order to earn a living, and he supplemented his earnings with private performances, music lessons and the publication of his work.

And work it was. Although the wunderkind was blessed with prodigious gifts of invention and quick to formulate musical ideas in his head, he was slow to get these ideas down on paper and fully notate his musical scores.

On top of this, Mozart and his fellow composers were newly responsible for their own fame and fortune. Various circumstances, such as increasing urbanisation and the beginning of the Industrial Revolution, meant that the established system of patronage, in which composers served the musical demands of aristocratic households, was falling into decline. In its stead came a commercially driven musical culture, targeted at the ever more prosperous and educated middle classes. With their newfound independence, yet without today's array of publicists, press officers, managers and agents, composers made their services available – at a price.

This price was important to Mozart. 'My desire and my hope,' he wrote in May 1781, 'is to gain honour, fame and money.' A few days later he added: 'Believe me, my sole purpose is to make as much money as possible, for after good health it is the best thing to have.'

Obligation came with it. Mozart knew that in order to secure further commissions, and thus further income, he needed to satisfy the demands of his employers and his audience. He revealed as much in a letter to his father, written in 1778 from Paris, where his latest symphony had just been premiered by a prestigious concert society:

> I prayed to God that it might go well. In the middle of the first [movement] there was a passage that I felt sure must please. The audience was quite carried away – and there was a tremendous burst of applause. ... I was so happy that as soon as the symphony was over I went off to the Palais Royal, where I had a large ice, said the rosary as I had vowed to do – and went home.

He went on to describe how his audience had made shushing noises during a quiet passage of the symphony, then clapped enthusiastically in the middle of a movement. Such behaviour was typical. Concertgoers of the period would often act informally during performances, conducting their social life as enthusiastically as listening to music. Even Mozart's.

There'll be more on audiences and concert-going later (clapping in the middle of a movement?!) but for the moment let's just reflect on these few home truths: Mozart was a public artist; he composed for a marketplace that could make or break his career; his music was designed to entertain; and he was genuinely overjoyed when it did so.

It's difficult, then, to concur with the so-called connoisseurs, to uphold their belief in the otherworldliness of classical music. As far as Mozart is concerned, the evidence suggests the opposite – that both he and his music were thoroughly entrenched in the real world. The composer was subject to the demands of his employers, and to the tastes and trends of his public. Concert-going, in Mozart's lifetime, was a social activity, an opportunity for people to meet, chat and conduct their business in public. And as for Mozart's music, the composer often borrowed from the popular music of the day, peppering his instrumental works and his operas with the characteristic rhythms of social dances such as the minuet, the polonaise and the gigue.

So, all hail *Hooked on Classics*! It seems the album shouldn't be written off as a caricature, a ridiculous attempt to rebrand classical music as cheesy 1980s pop. Rather, it should remind us of something that flies in the face of customary musical snobbery: that classical music and pop music are closely related. The history of the one involves the history of the other; their roots have been entangled from the beginning.

Mozart's is not the only classical music that aligns with the popular, although it may well be the most obvious: like today's stars of pop and jazz, Mozart had a habit of ad-libbing, making up music on the spot, usually at the keyboard. This helps explain the recent influx of Mozart 'crossovers' – attempts, post *Hooked on Classics*, to infuse Mozart's music with popular styles and idioms. A particular favourite of mine is the 2009 album *Mozart's Blue Dreams*, the brainchild of American trumpeter Joe Burgstaller and Grammy-nominated pianist Hector Martignon. Like *Hooked on Classics*, this album adapts Mozart's 'Turkish March', the finale of his Sonata in A Major, K. 331. (The K number, by the way, refers to the chronological catalogue of Mozart's compositions that was created in 1862 by the scholar Ludwig von Köchel.) With Burgstaller and Martignon, though, disco is swapped for shuffle and strut, jazz idioms that turn Mozart's march into what sounds like a loose-limbed striptease. Watch out for the trumpet growls.

Also watch out for Burgstaller's home-made music video, for the action is not a little symbolic. Burgstaller is in bed, snoring loudly to the sounds of classical Mozart. An alarm bell rings. It flashes fluorescent blue. Waking up, Burgstaller grabs his trumpet. (It is lying beside him under his duvet.) He gets out of bed and starts to play jazzed-up Mozart, his schmoozy phrases accompanied by an unseen piano, double bass and drum kit. Classical Mozart is confined to night-time slumber. New Mozart, injected with a dose of swing, is for the breaking day.

.

*Even before the music
begins there is that bored
look on people's faces.
A polite form of self-imposed
torture, the concert.*
HENRY MILLER

Concert halls?
Blow 'em up!

I ADMIT I'VE STOLEN the idea. In the 1960s the French conductor and composer Pierre Boulez urged that opera houses should be blown up. They were, he said, old-fashioned and obsolete, unsuited to both new operas and new productions of old. But here's a thought: why not get rid of concert halls too? Not because of any outdated or inappropriate décor, and not even because of possible acoustic deficiencies or restrictions of space. The problem with concert halls is that they may not promote a healthy musical environment and help us on our way towards a genuine and imaginative encounter with music.

Concert halls are dark. They have no windows. They are designed so that we, the audience, can't see outside, can't sense the passing of time or be disturbed by any external stimuli. So we sit, often cramped and uncomfortable, wearing fancy outfits that weren't supposed to get creased. And for the duration of the concert we keep our natural bodily processes in check: we don't (daren't) cry, laugh, call out or mutter, and of course we don't move. Chances are each of us feels self-conscious, not to mention alone. Stuck on a seat in the dark, we may not know the people around us; in the shadowy surrounds, we may not even recognise our companions. Faces are obscured. Bodies are lifeless. We are trapped in the concert hall coffin.

Yes, I know this account is grim. And I know, even as I write, that there are people who take pleasure in concert-going and wouldn't have their musical fix any other way. Yet I can't help thinking how strange it is that music – so alive, so effervescent – is cooped up in a place that is dead and ultimately detached from the world. And this is to say nothing of the audiences, with our controlled emotions and cool demeanour. Are we dead and detached too?

First, a bit of history. The concert hall, with its social etiquette and silent ritual, dates from the late eighteenth century. This was an important period in European music history, one that witnessed what's known as the 'great divide' between musical styles and purposes. Before this, music was composed and performed mainly for specific functions and settings – social and domestic gatherings, religious ceremonies and other public events. You might think of George Frideric Handel's *Music for the Royal Fireworks*, composed to celebrate the signing of the Treaty of Aix-la-Chapelle in 1748. Or J.S. Bach's *Musical Offering*, presented to King Frederick II of Prussia the year before.

Serving a practical purpose, this specially composed music was heard by listeners most often engaged in something else – an act of worship or a dance, a festive dinner party, an evening soirée, a fireworks show.

In the late eighteenth century, a new type of music began to emerge. 'Absolute' music, as historians like to call it, was autonomous and self-sufficient; it had no specific social milieu and no purpose other than sound. Purely for the ears, this music became an object of almost religious reverence, held in the highest esteem by listeners engaged, not in praying, dancing, chatting or eating, but in listening and nothing else.

The history of the symphony is telling in this regard. Once a kind of aristocratic party music, the genre became synonymous with music as 'art', pure aesthetic experience. The new symphonic music was associated with typically Romantic ideals of spirituality and transcendence. Supposedly free from the mundane realities of worldly life, it found a home in the concert hall – and set about teaching audiences how to behave.

That we've learned our lesson is obvious. When the lights are dimmed we sit still and shut up. Even in a full hall we are effectively in solitude. And then there is the passive aggression: anger directed at fidgety fingers and chesty coughs, and furious stares cast at children acting up – acting, well, like children. Only the other day a colleague of mine wanted to strangle a couple of twitchy toddlers. 'They should be locked up,' he said, adding, 'I blame the parents.'

Less hard-nosed was the Slovakian violist who, when his solo performance was interrupted by that god-awful Nokia ringtone, threw an annoyed glance at his audience, paused a moment, then performed an improvisation on the mobile jingle.

Hats off to him. Although initially put out, the violist exchanged his annoyance for a moment of musical wit, a classy comeback that caused the audience to laugh out loud. Hats off to them, for when was the last time anything actually happened in a concert hall? When was the last laugh, the last cry, the last murmur of discontent? The sanctified space of the hall, it seems, has deadened our senses. We're so dosed up on etiquette that only an elegy to a ringtone can provoke a response.

The improvisation went viral. A YouTube sensation, some say it was deliberately staged by Nokia in an attempt to revive interest in the iPhone-eclipsed brand. Whatever the case, the episode is worth mulling over because it makes us think about what goes on in a concert hall and what does not, what we tolerate and what we do not, and how our ideas and expectations might be overturned entirely, or at least challenged a little.

A few years ago I was at a performance in London of the 1913 ballet *The Rite of Spring*, a work well known for its raucous Paris premiere. Countless books and essays have documented the riot that occurred during this first performance, reporting who said what, where, when and why – why Igor Stravinsky's music, or Vaslav Nijinsky's choreography, caused such a commotion, and why the audience scoffed and booed. Some flung objects at the stage. Others walked out.

According to acclaimed music historian Richard Taruskin, the riot remains the most spectacular event in music history. It certainly seems worth mentioning here. Remember the spectators, far from passive or respectful? They might teach us a thing or two not only about historical attitudes to music, but about passion and engagement, and their place in the listening experience.

For better or worse, there was no riot during the London performance I attended. Nonetheless, from my seat in the stalls of the Lilian Baylis Studio, Sadler's Wells, I witnessed the strangest of scenes, and one that unsettled my understanding of concert-hall conventions.

A man, alone on the concert platform, casually dressed in T-shirt and jeans, jumped up and down, flailing his arms and twisting his body into exaggerated, unnatural shapes. He looked to be possessed. Directly facing the audience, he had no props. His only companion was Stravinsky's music. Twenty-four channels — a recording of the Berlin Philharmonic under Simon Rattle — blared from speakers dotted around the hall.

At one point, in the midst of his abrupt jerking, the man stared at me — stared right through me, it felt. Oddly, he seemed convinced that I had an oboe. He pointed to me while 'cuing' the oboe entries; he caught my eye and emphatically beat time.

It wasn't just me he singled out. When clarinets could be heard on the recording moments later, the man gestured to some people sitting behind me. He appeared to make eye contact with them too. We all shuffled in our seats, unsure what was going on. Why was he looking at us?

Stranger still, the music started to repeat. Familiar with the score, I noticed that an entire section was played twice, yet the man continued to writhe around, seemingly oblivious to the musical repetition. Then he stopped abruptly. He lowered his arms, wiped his brow and walked to the side of the stage. He paced around for a few moments, visibly relaxing. He seemed happy to have a breather, to let the music continue on its own.

Only for a couple of minutes, though. Revving himself up, he returned to the centre of the stage, looked the audience in the eye and continued to gesticulate wildly.

The man was Xavier Le Roy, a microbiologist turned choreographer and leading figure within contemporary conceptual art. The performance was a typical Le Roy mind-bender, a deliberate attempt to bamboozle the audience and make us wonder what on earth was going on.

Having watched documentary footage of Rattle and the Berlin Phil, Le Roy wanted to emulate the conductor's movements, to convey similar animation and physical energy while directing his own (unseen) orchestra. Yet he also wanted to dance, to react to the orchestral music he was, simultaneously, engineering. His movements, then, were not only the 'cause' of the music, they were an 'effect' of it. Like a hot rod poking into his body, the music made him leap and jerk and lurch and hop and jolt and wrench and wriggle.

This confusion of music and movement was not Le Roy's only initiative. Equally unconventional, and equally confusing, was his manipulation of the concert-hall space. Facing the stalls, he engaged with his audience, inviting us to play a part in the musical performance. If Le Roy had a dual identity, as both conductor and dancer, so did we. We were both listeners – still, silent, and sitting in rows – and members of the orchestra, beckoned into the musical sphere.

Involving the audience, enlivening the atmosphere, transforming the way we looked and listened: Le Roy achieved all this within the confines of the concert hall. Like the ballet's premiere almost a century earlier, the Frenchman's performance provoked a new kind of audience interaction, one that upturned the traditionally restrained and contemplative mode of listening. As on May 29, 1913, when hats were flung and expletives yelled, a new type of concert-hall experience had come into being.

Besides that evening in London, I've had the privilege of attending a couple of other performances of *The Rite of Spring* that flouted concert-hall conventions. One, also in London, was at the newly refurbished Royal Festival Hall on the South Bank. It was what you might call a 3-D extravaganza. While listening to Stravinsky's score played live by the London Philharmonic, we watched the dancing of soloist Julia Mach, projected on to a giant screen. (Mach was actually dancing in a black box at the side of the stage.) It was the strangest concert-hall experience I've ever had. We were wearing those ugly 3-D glasses, so Mach's every move seemed almost nauseating: too real, too close, too personal.

The other performance, at Auckland's Aotea Centre, featured neither a giant screen nor a solo dancer. Instead, 190 young people danced on stage, directed by a British choreographer, Royston Maldoom. To Stravinsky's music, performed by the Auckland Philharmonia Orchestra at the front of the stage, rather than in the usual concert position, the dancers brought to life a story quite unlike the Russian original, with its scenes of pagan ritual and sacrifice. Maldoom's version enacted the voyaging of Māori across the South Pacific, but the story was not the only intriguing element: the dancers were schoolchild-ren, untrained and from a cross-section of society.

Known affectionately as the Pied Piper of dance, Maldoom had an explicit social agenda. He certainly wanted to entertain his young dancers, giving them the opportunity to rehearse and perform in a professional venue and to the accompaniment of a live orchestra. But he also believed that by dancing together to the strains of Stravinsky's music they would experience a kind of physical, emotional and spiritual uplift. So convinced was Maldoom of the educational value of his project that he took it all over the globe. His *Rite of Spring* has been performed, to different dramatic scenarios, by children in Ethiopia, Peru, Germany, the United Kingdom, Northern Ireland, South Africa, and the United States, as well as New Zealand.

That evening in Auckland, Maldoom's social commit-ment re-energised my concert-hall experience. The atmosphere inside the Aotea Centre was carnivalesque – like being at a festival, a street party, even a football match. So much for classical music's supposed elitism, I found myself thinking. The musical experience is open to all. Professionals can share the spotlight with untrained children straight from school; connoisseurs of Stravinsky can applaud alongside proud parents and friends. Innate artistry, it seems, is within us all. And today's concert halls can channel it.

Music is always migrating from its points of origin to its destiny in someone's fleeting moment of experience.

ALEX ROSS

Journeyers

NOT LONG AFTER ARRIVING in Auckland to take up a position at the university's school of music, I flew south to Wellington to attend an evening concert by the New Zealand Symphony Orchestra. The journey was memorable, as much for the plane's turbulent landing (typical, I'm told) as for my in-flight celebrity-spotting. To my left sat a world-renowned fashion designer, and a few seats behind an unkempt All Black.

Even more memorable was the concert itself. This came as something of a surprise, as I wasn't at all enthusiastic about the programme. It followed a standard –

some might say stale – musical structure. There was the customary Show-Stopper: the well-known and well-liked piece at the end of the programme that enjoyed top billing on posters, flyers and ads. Stopping the show, on this occasion, was Igor Stravinsky's *Firebird.* On billboards across the city, the title was accompanied by a flame-haired model and the teaser 'Ignite the fire inside'.

Also on the programme was the traditional Show-Off: the piece chosen to flaunt the musical skills of the orchestra and/or soloist. Tone, lyricism, technical ability, expression, character, confidence and poise – these were all to be applauded, that evening, in the performance by mezzo-soprano Sasha Cooke of Gustav Mahler's late nineteenth-century *Songs of a Wayfarer*.

Then there was the third piece, the Show-Us-What-You're-Made-Of. This type of piece tends to be challenging to play, as well as challenging to listen to. Performers and audience need to dig deep into their musical knowledge and experience to grasp the real substance of the work. Douglas Lilburn's Symphony No. 3 fitted the bill nicely. The lesser-known symphony by the so-called grandfather of New Zealand music is not only stubbornly resistant to easy listening, it also shows the concert-going public just what that music is made of – its characteristic styles, sounds and orchestral effects.

To my mind, then, the fare was not a little formulaic. The three pieces conformed to standard musical types that, when programmed together, seemed able to satisfy both artistic/serious and commercial/crowd-pleasing imperatives.

Equally formulaic, I couldn't help but think, were the programme notes. I have never been a fan of these mini essays available for purchase, often at considerable expense, before a performance. Yes, they can provide something to read (when waiting for a concert to begin), something to pretend to read (when alone), or something to busy your hands with (when bored).

And yes, they can tell us a thing or two: in this case that Mahler's *Songs* are about the sadness and sorrow of a man lamenting his lost love; that Stravinsky's *Firebird* is about good versus evil (the downfall of a green-taloned ogre called Kashchei and the victory of the glittering Firebird); and that Lilburn's third symphony is about, well, nothing at all – this being quite odd for the composer, as I'll explain in a moment. But all this information can be found online quite easily, and at no cost. Indeed, chances are the online sources will be less dreary and off-putting than the usual programme notes, packed with jargon and dry historical facts.

Interestingly, too, programme notes are a contradiction in terms. They should really be called 'piece notes' since they tell us less about a programme – that is, a carefully conceived compilation of music – than about individual pieces, seemingly separate, stand-alone items.

Standing alone, myself, in the foyer of the Michael Fowler Centre, the Wellington home of the NZSO, I turned my attention to the orchestral brochure, a glitzy guide to the 2012 season. Immediately I was intrigued. As well as the usual lists of concert repertoire, venues and dates, there were double-page full-colour images of the orchestral musicians, dramatically posed against computer-generated, digitally enhanced landscapes. These landscapes were not only visually impressive, they were inspired by the music to be performed that season. Stretches of desert and towering pyramids set the scene for Saint-Saëns's Piano Concerto No. 5 (dubbed the 'Egyptian'). Lush green hills and precipitous cliffs depicted Mendelssohn's *Hebrides Overture*.

But the images brought to life more than individual pieces of music. They achieved what programme notes tend not to: they took in all the music of the concert. The Hebrides scene, for example, featured a cellist dressed as a soldier, linking Mendelssohn's overture to the piece it would accompany on the March programme – Edward Elgar's Cello Concerto, written towards the end of the First World War and often described as an elegy to its victims.

The Egyptian sands were home to a huge bust of Shostakovich, coupling Saint-Saëns's 'Egyptian' concerto with its two concert bedfellows in May – the monument to Russian nationalism that is Shostakovich's Fifth Symphony and a monument of a different kind, Anthony Ritchie's orchestral piece *Diary of a Madman: Dedication to Shostakovich.*

This linking of repertoire was endorsed in the brochure by several quotations from the NZSO's musical director, Finnish conductor Pietari Inkinen. To Inkinen, a concert programme is more than the sum of its parts. It's a coherent entity, a dramatic scenario, an odyssey. The orchestral musicians, Inkinen quipped, were 'seasoned explorers ... hard-wired to seek adventure'. The audience, too, were journeyers: 'Every concert is a voyage and, like all travel experiences, you're transformed as you arrive home. What you've encountered has enriched you beyond measure, and you'll never be quite the same again.'

Loitering in the foyer, I was quite taken by Inkinen's idea that listening to a concert – even in a traditional venue – could be an invigorating experience, and that a concert programme – even one with a traditional structure – could have a dramatic theme, an unfolding musical narrative. I decided to put the idea to the test that evening. I would take on the role of journeyer and navigate through the programme. With those digital images firmly in mind, I wondered about the musical landscapes I would encounter on my travels. And I wondered how to join the dots on the concert's musical map.

Lilburn's Symphony No. 3 – the first piece on the programme – sounds quite unlike the rest of the composer's orchestral repertoire. His first two symphonies, the *Drysdale Overture*, the *Festival Overture* and the symphonic poems *Aotearoa*, *Forest* and *A Song of Islands*, all represent, in the words of one critic, 'the elevating power of the New Zealand landscape'. It's almost impossible to hear this music without imagining the country's natural beauties: the mountainous terrain, the steep-sided valleys, the rivers, streams, seas, peaks, gorges, bush and beaches. 'Paradise' was the word used by Lilburn to describe his childhood home, Drysdale, an isolated hillside farm in the central North Island. And paradise is what we hear. The *Drysdale Overture* is wonderfully evocative, its lean melodies tracing the contours of the countryside, and chirpy woodwind solos depicting Lilburn's boyish escapades in the bush.

The third symphony, completed in 1961, is something else entirely. 'Quite a departure,' said Robert Burch, a horn player in the orchestra that premiered the work. 'Douglas had changed course at least 90 degrees.'

Lilburn himself may have agreed, for he described the symphony as 'harsh', 'didactic' and 'personalised'. It does indeed seem harsh. Jagged rhythms drive the music forward. Repeated again and again, these rhythms grind away at the ear — and the nerves — with their spikiness and intensity. 'Didactic' seems about right, too. The symphony is based on the atonal musical language that Lilburn had studied abroad, a language centred on neither the traditional major nor minor scales but on the entire spectrum of chromatic notes (the black and white keys on a piano).

As for 'personalised', it was only as the music was coming to an end that this word began to ring true. Listening to the symphony, I realised, was like listening to Lilburn himself. It was as if the composer had sat himself on a psychiatrist's couch, expressed and observed his thoughts and feelings, and then transcribed the entire deposition for orchestra.

When Lilburn composed this piece, you see, he'd reached something of a crisis in his career, a point from which he would never turn back. During various overseas trips he'd been exposed to the latest trends in musical composition. Now, back in New Zealand, he was grappling with what he had learned.

From the English composer Ralph Vaughan-Williams, Lilburn knew to follow his intuition, to let his imagination run wild and free. From the German innovator Karlheinz Stockhausen, he had become aware of the technique known as 'serialism', a mathematical ordering system for musical pitch. And from the classical composers whose music he had long adored, he knew to be humble, and not a little insecure. 'I'd grown up with the idea that all music had been written by great masters a hundred years before, overseas,' Lilburn said in an interview, 'and I didn't know whether anyone was allowed to do it here in New Zealand.'

Symphony No. 3, then, is a self-portrait in sound. The acerbic rhythms, prickly motifs, unsettled chords, unblended sounds, agitated melodies, stream-of-consciousness musical structure and general turbulence are the results of Lilburn's training and his assimilation of different techniques. But they also speak of a man who is anxious and unsure, not only about his music but about his role and legitimacy as a composer – a composer from an isolated farm in a no-man's-land at the edge of the world.

As the symphony ended, the obvious point came to mind: Lilburn, like me that evening, was on a journey. He'd travelled extensively throughout his life, roaming through native bush as a child, visiting Europe as a student, taking sabbaticals overseas during his tenure at Wellington's Victoria University. And here he was, in his third symphony, travelling still. In this piece, his last excursion with traditional instruments (from now on he would compose only electronic music), he flies on the wings of the orchestra, hovering over the musical territories he has encountered on his travels.

Travelling, journeying, wandering, roaming: the metaphor was to become important. Next on the programme was *Songs of a Wayfarer*, a song cycle composed by the Austrian Gustav Mahler in the mid 1880s, following the breakup of his love affair with the singer Johanna Richter. These four songs, the first in particular, are gloomy. At a slow pace and in a minor key, the opening vocal melody never quite seems to get going. It hovers around one note, then tries to reach higher and higher but ends up falling back on itself, descending through a sequence of what are known as 'sigh' figures — a kind of musical onomatopoeia.

Adding to the gloomy mood is the meagre symphonic accompaniment. Violins mirror the vocal line, never straying from the solemn melody, while a solitary note on the cellos and basses reverberates around the largely silent orchestra. Bowed repeatedly — it's called a pulsed pedal or drone — this low note creates an impression of stasis, of time standing still. There's no sense of progression or forward thrust, merely the prolongation of a single chord.

All this gloominess befits the lyrics of the song: 'When my darling has her wedding day, her joyous wedding day, I will have my day of mourning! I will go to my little room, my dark little room, and weep, weep for my darling, for my dear darling!'

This is depressing stuff, so you might not expect the musical jingle that appears at the start of the song and repeats throughout. Played fairly quickly by clarinets, harp and triangle, this jingle sounds frivolous, jaunty and almost banal. It's as if Mahler is playing 'peep-po' with his audience.

The jingle may, though, be dramatically appropriate, because just as the singer laments his lost love, describing her 'joyous' wedding day, the music of the wedding band interjects, its sparkling percussion and sprightly clarinets evoking a festive atmosphere.

What the song presents, then, is a dramatic dissonance: the wedding music intrudes into the protagonist's
interior reverie; the jingle undercuts the solemn and sor-
rowful atmosphere. This head-butting of moods – the
silly and the serious, the comic and the contemplative –
continues throughout the song cycle, throwing the vocal
line into dramatic relief and emphasising the loss and isolation of the Wayfarer.

The character of the Wayfarer, incidentally, is a legacy
of the nineteenth century: social outcasts, vagabonds,
nomads and wanderers were ubiquitous in Romantic
prose fiction. Works by some of the most prominent
writers of the time – Goethe, Heine, Wordsworth, Balzac,
Flaubert and Mary Shelley – featured various 'figures of
mobility' (as one critic called them), all searching to
make sense of life, to find a voice and a place among
societies both familiar and foreign. Mahler's singing
Wayfarer is no exception. In the composer's words, he is
'stricken by fate ... he now sets forth into the world,
travelling wherever his road may lead him'.

I now settled back to hear the third item on the
programme, Stravinsky's *Firebird*, an orchestral score
composed in 1910 as the accompaniment to a ballet. Born
in Russia in 1882, Igor Stravinsky, like Douglas Lilburn,
travelled widely. He lived in France, went into exile in
Switzerland, and in 1940, a few months after the
outbreak of the Second World War, he moved to the

United States. As a musician, Stravinsky was defined by his émigré status: he was almost always an outsider, looking in on society, trying to find ways to communicate – through music – with different foreign audiences.

With *Firebird*, Stravinsky got lucky. The success of the ballet, a production by the Paris-based Ballets Russes, thrust the composer into the international spotlight. But there was one problem. Under the influence of the ballet impresario Sergei Diaghilev, Stravinsky had been implored to create a specifically Russian-sounding score, one that conveyed the exoticism, splendour and mystery that European audiences associated with that country's impassioned and indulgent spirit. The vivid orchestration, folk-like melodies, flickering harmonies and frenzied rhythms, all hallmarks of Stravinsky's style, certainly sounded Russian to Parisian audiences in 1910, and they still sound Russian today. But their authenticity is dubious. Stravinsky's score may tell us less about real-life Russian styles than about music designed to appeal to Western notions of Russia, its art, culture and folklore.

Stravinsky, Lilburn, Mahler's Wayfarer: all three were journeyers. They travelled far and wide, experiencing isolation and loneliness. And they navigated difficult terrain, often seeking to reconcile personal needs and desires with circumstances over which they had no control: the demands of a difficult impresario; the teaching of foreign musical masters; the loss of a lover.

If I hadn't been on my own journey that evening, plotting a course through the concert programme, I might not have made these connections. I might have heard three different and seemingly unrelated pieces. I might well have become bored. So I flew out of Wellington with a new-found respect for concert programmes and, glass of wine in hand, I toasted the orchestra's behind-the-scenes team who had planned the concert.

At the same time, I knew my interpretation of the concert was precisely that, my own. As Lilburn himself once said: 'Nobody translates the messages which come through the ears in quite the same way.'

I had a final thought. Classical concerts may be poorly attended, as people often complain, but they may also be poorly attended *to* – that is, poorly heard. I'm not going to promote the sort of dutiful reverence or analytical attention that some think is necessary when listening to classical music. I'd rather suggest something less orthodox. When you're at a concert, let your imagination roam freely across the programme, tracing a visionary path through piece after piece after piece. Go on your own journey. You may be surprised where it leads.

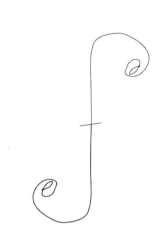

Truth is a great flirt.

FRANZ LISZT

Confessions

I N THE LATE FOURTH CENTURY, a bishop called Augustine, who was later declared a saint, penned what is now considered to be the first autobiography. *Confessions*, one of Augustine's many surviving writings, recounts the author's conversion to Christianity. (In his youth, Augustine had led an errant life, indulging in pagan philosophy and sex out of wedlock.) But *Confessions* also tells a story about music and how we should hear it, a story that resonates today.

Recalling his journey to faith, Augustine describes the joy he felt on hearing music sung in church. He was 'deeply moved', 'enthralled', and reduced to 'tears of gladness' by the communal singing of what would have been simple, slow-paced, undulating melodies. The proper term for these melodies is chants, from *cantus*, the Latin word for song. Unaccompanied and sung in unison, these early Christian chants pre-date the Gregorian chants of the medieval period. The Gregorian repertoire, supposedly invented by Pope Gregory I and set to the official texts of the Mass, was not standardised or notated in any way until early in the nineteenth century.

Like his Christian brothers, Augustine believed that music could hold sway over the emotions. In a church service, sung hymns and psalms could enhance the religious experience, helping to revive tired souls, increase passion and piety, and further the praise of God. But the intensity of emotion aroused by music caused Augustine some concern. Feelings of pleasure and joy might arouse the congregation, especially the weaker spirits among it, but they might also paralyse their minds. Enjoying church music without attending to the meaning of the words being sung – gratifying the senses without applying the mind – was a grave danger, a 'grievous sin'. It was a sin that Augustine felt compelled to confess, asking his readers and God himself for pity and mercy.

You will no doubt recognise the tension Augustine describes – between listening for pleasure and listening for some sort of intellectual or spiritual improvement. Over almost two millennia it's become characteristic of

Western thinking, not only about church music but about classical music more broadly. Concert halls, as I mentioned earlier, have the effect of smothering our sensory responses to music. Our bodies feel paralysed; diversions are suppressed. The message we get is that we should listen carefully for our education and enlightenment, rather than simply for fun.

Certainly, this tension – philosophers may say it's a tension between body and mind, between primal instincts and cultivated knowledge – is familiar to me. Like Augustine, I've often felt uneasy when listening to classical music purely for kicks. (Even the phrase sounds wrong in this context.) A voice inside my head tells me that I'm not paying enough attention to the music, that I'm disrespecting the composer and his or her intentions.

Perhaps, like Augustine, I should make a confession: I like to practise yoga to fifteenth-century church music. I do the ironing to Guiseppe Verdi's *Requiem Mass*. I regularly listen to Johannes Brahms' four symphonies while lying in the bath. And I have been known to get myself psyched up – for exams, important meetings, even for cleaning the oven – with the help of Dmitri Shostakovich.

During these activities, my mind isn't working – at least not in the music-analytical manner it's been trained to adopt. But a series of questions does spring up. Why am I listening to this music? What purpose is it serving? And what does it mean that I've chosen it – and that, however many years after it came into existence, it is able to take on new functions and meanings?

These questions seem worth pursuing because it's all too easy to succumb to that critical inner voice. And it's even easier to *be* that voice, making sweeping assertions about the general irreverence of today's listeners. What's harder – yet so much more worthwhile – is to try to account for our musical choices. I'll have a go here, doing some detective work into my favourite yoga soundtrack.

Missa Prolationum is the Latin name for the Prolation Mass, an unaccompanied choral work by the Franco-Flemish singer and composer Johannes Ockeghem. Written around 1460, this peculiarly titled composition (I'll say more about the title later) was originally performed in the chapel of the French royal court, where Ockeghem served for nearly half a century.

Ockeghem's Mass – comprising the standard five sections: Kyrie, Gloria, Credo, Sanctus and Agnus Dei – is often regarded as a high point in fifteenth-century church music, a masterpiece of vocal splendour and intensity. Partly this is to do with vocal range, the range of pitches (from lowest to highest) a given vocal part can sing. Each of the usual four parts – soprano, alto, tenor and bass – covers a wider range than was customary for the period. This results in an especially rich musical sound, particularly at the lower end of each vocal range, where the parts tend to blur and criss-cross.

Also remarkable is the lack of a single melody and accompaniment. Instead, the four parts appear to be of equal importance, sharing material — interesting rhythms, melodic figures — among themselves.

Then there are the long-breathed phrases, unravelling continuously in each part. At the very outset, several phrases are composed from only two words ('Kyrie, eleison', Lord, have mercy). The syllables are stretched, sung to two, three, four or more notes, sometimes whole cascades of notes. These tumbling phrases tend to proceed by step, moving from one note to the next, and rarely jump up or down more than a few steps. In fact, several rise and then fall, as if trying to emulate the characteristic arch of a medieval church vault.

Silky smooth and mellifluous, the opening Kyrie illustrates the polyphonic (many voices) style for which Ockeghem was and still is known. But this is to say nothing of the music's most distinctive feature, which is that the Kyrie is constructed as a canon or round: a single part is echoed and overlapped by another. In fact, the movement is made up of two canons unfolding simultaneously: the alto imitates the soprano, while the bass imitates the tenor. Yet this is not your simple note-by-note imitation, the kind familiar to us from children's songs such as 'London's Burning' and 'Frère Jacques'. With Ockeghem, the imitating voices do so at different speeds. One part sings the same notes as another, but proceeds at a slower rate, lengthening each syllable, prolonging each phrase.

The other movements of the Mass are constructed in the same manner, although there's a small but significant difference. In the opening Kyrie the imitation occurs 'at the unison': the imitating voice sings exactly the same pitches as the original. In the next movement the imitation is 'at the second': the imitating voice sings one step higher, at the interval of a second. The next is 'at the third', the next 'at the fourth', and so on. The result is a compositional tour de force, an elaborate network of canons that proceed systematically through different intervals and speeds.

Let's pause for a moment and ask a seemingly mundane question. What does any of this have to offer my yoga practice? I certainly don't listen out for all those canons. Indeed, I wonder if anyone does – come to think of it, if anyone can. Historians have suggested that even the fifteenth-century congregation, Ockeghem's original audience, would have had a hard time following the music. For the canons were bizarre technical trickery: their only purpose seems to have been to flaunt the composer's oh-so-clever craftsmanship.

Although I can't make out all the canons, the overall echo effect creates a ceaselessly flowing sound. As the voices imitate each other, their phrases interweave and overlap. This means there are few obvious points of rest, places where all the phrases come to an end and all the voices unite – the musical equivalent of a full stop.

This, for me, is one of the music's main attractions. Knitted together and never seeming to end, Ockeghem's phrases encourage me to stretch that bit further, to hold the stretch that bit longer. What's more, they help me transition seamlessly from one pose to the next.

My teacher is always telling me that the key to yoga is 'time in the pose'. Ockeghem makes me take that time, even when my hamstrings or quads or glutes or biceps are screaming. But it's not only the overlapping phrases I have to thank. The impression of time standing still – of one continuous, prolonged musical moment – is also the result of the composer's handling of metre.

In contemporary music theory, metre refers to a regular pattern of beats or pulses, a pattern that plays out once per bar (a bar being a unit of time) and is indicated at the beginning of a piece by a time signature. You may already be familiar with the basics. Duple metre indicates two beats per bar and is identified by time signatures such as $\frac{2}{4}$ (two crotchets per bar) and $\frac{2}{2}$ (two minims per bar). Triple metre means three beats per bar and can be indicated by $\frac{3}{4}$ (three crotchets per bar) or $\frac{3}{8}$ (three quavers per bar)

Incidentally, crotchets, minims and quavers are types of note-value: they indicate the relative duration or length of a note. (Two crotchets occupy the same length of time as one minim; two quavers, one crotchet.) It's the combination of different note-values that creates rhythm.

There's another point to remember. Musical metre, as we understand it nowadays, implies stress or accent. The first beat of a bar is always strong (and is called the downbeat), while the second is weak and unaccented. The accent pattern of any further beat or beats depends on the number of beats per bar: for example, **1**, 2, **1**, 2 or **1**, 2, 3, **1**, 2, 3 or **1**, 2, 3, 4, **1**, 2, 3, 4.

In Ockeghem's day, however, metre meant something quite different. Music had rhythm, of course. Indeed, in the history of music, rhythm, based on the lengths of syllables of spoken verse, came first, before anyone thought of bars or time signatures. Fifteenth-century music such as Ockeghem's also had a beat, called a tactus. It was a 'felt' pulse, roughly equivalent to the human pulse when breathing normally. But there was no pattern of beats. There were no bars, and consequently no bar-lines, the vertical lines drawn through music's horizontal axis, the 'staff'. What's more, the strange-looking signs at the beginning of a piece didn't indicate the division of a unit of time into beats, like modern time signatures. They indicated the division of beats into note-values.

This dividing-up of the beat was called 'prolation', hence Ockeghem's 'Prolation Mass'. The choral work not only lacks the strong and weak accents so familiar to us today. Because the parts sing the same material but at different speeds – technically speaking at different prolations – the music also lacks any sense of regularity or patterning, any sense of metre in the modern meaning of the term. This isn't music that you can walk or dance to. You can't even beat time to it.

What you can do is float away on the soaring phrases. The music seems to reach for a higher plane or state of consciousness, somewhere beyond the material world. Listening to it reminds me of the words of my favourite poet, Charles Baudelaire:

> The contemplation of something infinitely large and infinitely beautiful, an intense light which delights the soul to the point of ecstasy or trance, and finally the sensation of space expanded to the furthest limits of the imagination.

Baudelaire, writing in April 1861, is describing the music of the German composer Richard Wagner – music that, when you hear it, is not unlike Ockeghem's in its unending phrases and overall expansiveness. In February 1860 Baudelaire had written Wagner a letter, expressing admiration for his music. He had continued to ponder that music throughout the year, debating what to make of it, what to learn from it, and how he, as a literary man, might best describe it in words. In the end it took him over a year to produce a now infamous essay in which he grappled with the relation between Wagner's music and his own artistic endeavours.

Baudelaire's prolonged and intense engagement with Wagner offers an interesting lesson. If we leave classical music alone, locked in an ivory tower, it becomes a kind of monologue imposed from on high. But if we welcome it into our world, engage with it, discuss it and debate it, we inject it with new energy and meaning.

Baudelaire, I'm sure, knew this. He knew he had to think long and hard about Wagner's music if he wanted that music to speak to a generation of writers, artists and critics. Ockeghem probably knew it too. His canons may well have evoked a spiritual mysticism perfected suited to the religious purpose of the Mass, but they would also be pored over and scrutinised, if not by the congregation itself then by fellow and future composers, not to mention (as I can attest) students of music theory several centuries later.

One question, then, remains. Will we keep the dialogue with this music going?

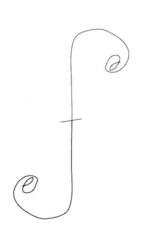

In music, things don't get
better or worse: they evolve
and transform themselves.
LUCIANO BERIO

Modern
classical

S O FAR THIS BOOK has been about breathing new life into the traditional classical repertoire. But let's spare a thought for the music composed in more recent times. To the English musician Brian Eno, this music – let's call it 'modern classical' – is best understood as a sort of scientific research. 'You're glad someone's done it,' Eno said in a 1990 interview with radio presenter Robert Sandall, 'but you don't necessarily want to listen to it.' He went on: 'It's similar to the way I'm very happy that people have gone to the North Pole. It extends my concept of the planet to know it exists, but I don't want to live there, or even to go there actually.'

Eno's view is one of the more sympathetic. Many devotees of classical music would prefer to trek north with ice axes and crampons than journey into the sound worlds of, say, Mauricio Kagel, György Ligeti or Iannis Xenakis.

Chances are you haven't heard of these composers, let alone heard their music. Years of living, breathing, seeing and hearing have taught us that much 'modern' art — whether it's music, painting, sculpture or poetry — is unashamedly mute. I don't mean mute in the literal sense, although one piece of music famously is. (More on this later.) I mean mute as in irrelevant and inexpressive, unable to communicate in conventional terms.

And let's be honest, some modern classical music can be pretty unpleasant to listen to, as well as difficult to follow. Often we don't get it. Rarely do we like it. So we tend not to bother with it at all.

Various strategies have been used to tempt us: careful concert programming (coupling a modern piece with a much loved masterwork); giving out freebies (pizza and beer at Chicago Symphony Orchestra concerts); after-concert parties (hosted by Milwaukee-based Present Music, one of the world's leading contemporary ensembles).

Even physical coercion has been attempted. Back in 1966 the American composer Max Neuhaus asked his Manhattan audience to exit the concert hall and meet him on a street corner. There he rubber-stamped

'LISTEN' on each person's hand and led them on a musical journey through New York City streets.

Less extreme was my experience with three different, although decidedly modern, classical pieces. First, a work with the humdrum title *Three Compositions for Piano*, written in 1947 by Milton Babbitt, a renowned composer at Princeton University. Among Babbitt's earliest works, this set of piano solos is thought to showcase several characteristics of the composer's style.

Let's focus on 'Composition No. 1'. It begins fast and furious — too fast and too furious perhaps: the music sounds mechanically speeded up, as though someone has pushed the fast-forward button on a CD player. The flurry of notes has no discernible melody or accompaniment, and no clear pattern of events. It's impossible to predict what will happen next, where the music will go.

As the piece spurts forward, the rush of random pitches — some high, some low, some loud, some quiet — never seems to let up. The avalanche continues until suddenly, without warning, everything comes to a halt. The effect makes me think of a garden hose with a life of its own, caterpillaring around a lawn, spraying water in all directions. That is, until someone turns off the tap.

Our struggle to understand this music may have a simple explanation. Scientific research has shown that the human brain is ill-disposed to patternless musical chaos. Music theorists Fred Lerdahl and Ray Jackendoff argue that we respond best to ordered musical processes: an identifiable metre and pulse, with clear strong and weak beats; repeated rhythmic and melodic motifs; and an overall musical 'grammar' in which every note has a specified function. If these are absent, we have to make a superhuman effort to keep track of what's going on.

In response to this research, academics have followed in the footsteps of Dove® and campaigned for natural beauty. Andrew Mead, professor of music at Indiana University, exclaims that this music may be difficult, complex and austere, but 'it yields up beauty upon beauty to the engaged listener'. It possesses a 'sensuous' allure. Another scholar has even claimed to hear nature itself – forest thickets, rolling waves – under Babbitt's frazzled and frantic surface. Gulp.

Training, technique, beauty and brain cells: thinking about these topics doesn't affect how I experience Babbitt's piece. I'd rather run with my first impression: the music sounds like a racket.

Questions now tumble forth. So, if it sounds like a racket, what is its purpose? Why would a composer write music like this? Why would anyone want to hear it, let alone pay money for the privilege?

To the last question, Babbitt may have replied: 'Don't hear it. Steer clear. Leave the music well alone.' In a 1958 article entitled 'Who Cares If You Listen?', he declared that modern classical music should be withdrawn from the public sphere – from the concert hall, the marketplace, and even from the average Joe and Joanna.

Like Brian Eno, Babbitt compared his music – 'serious', 'advanced', 'specialised' – to scientific research. Both, he said, belonged in universities and research institutes; neither was for public consumption. You wouldn't expect a layperson to understand the latest developments in astrophysics, or a radio repairman to understand theoretical physics, so why would you assume that the general public should be able to appreciate modern classical music?

Babbitt also thought music should have the same intellectual precision as science, with a similarly rational and rigorous modus operandus. He developed a method, 'integral serialism', in which all musical components are subjected to a predetermined formula. 'Composition No. 1' provides a good example. Although the music may sound random to the ear, it has actually been composed according to a strict set of rules. The succession of pitches, rhythms, loud notes, quiet notes, high notes, low notes: everything is codified and consistently mathematical. Everything has a logical place in an overall complex of musical relations.

Listening to 'Composition No. 1' with Babbitt's ideas in mind, it's tempting to lambast the composer for such a self-absorbed and sanctimonious point of view. Harsher critics have attacked Babbitt for worse, arguing that his pompous attitude and impenetrable music have contributed to the marginalisation of modern classical fare from the second half of the twentieth century.

But should we be so critical? When Babbitt developed his compositional method and published his ideas in print, he was looking to question what music could do – how it could function and be heard. He wanted to innovate, to experiment in sound, yet he found himself working at a time, following the Second World War and in the thick of the Cold War, when artists were racked by doubts about their relevance and role.

On one hand, they were worried about the challenges posed by popular music and the commercial sphere. On the other, they felt increasingly anxious about art itself, particularly Western ideals of representation, expression, creative freedom and beauty. Had the horrors of war not overturned these ideals and questioned their very legitimacy? Who could maintain the value of artistic freedom and beauty in a world rocked by bombs and barbarism, a world in which personal expression, and even personal existence, were continually under threat?

The nature and purpose of art began to take on new meaning as artists turned to science for answers. Science seemed to be everything that art was not. It was built on hard facts, universal truths, rational systems and controls. It seemed to transcend the vulnerability and transience of life.

While painters tended towards 'ultra-rationalist abstraction', reducing visual objects to their bare bones, musicians began to experiment with mathematical formulas, inventing ways to control their music by denying their personal 'voice', forgoing their own creativity. The Italian composer Luciano Berio summed it up nicely when he spoke of composers 'writing music without being personally involved'.

Babbitt is the prime example. He was happy to hand over his music to the logic of a governing formula. He was happy, it seems, to de-compose.

It never stops surprising me how a few historical facts can shed light on modern classical music, and on how we feel when we encounter it. Armed with these facts, we can gain an insight into music's 'symptomology' (still thinking in terms of science), its secret motivating forces.

This is my experience with Babbitt. For better or worse, I'll probably never like his music, never enjoy hearing it, but I know that liking and enjoying are not the point. Babbitt's music is not designed to leave a rosy after-glow. It's not supposed to be conventionally expressive. (Remember the bland title?) There are rules to follow, results to be had: you could call it music-by-numbers.

Daring us to think – and to hear – differently is also the challenge laid down by my next piece, *4'33"*, written in 1952 by the American composer John Cage. I suspect you've heard of it: it's the famous silent piece that consists of nothing but actions. A player of an unspecified instrument walks on to a stage, signals the beginning and ending of three movements, accepts applause, then walks off. He or she plays no music, for the composer hasn't composed any. But the traditional concert protocol remains in force. Throughout the 'performance', which lasts four minutes and 33 seconds, we in the audience sit still and listen.

When I first encountered this piece as a teenager, I was utterly confused. I thought I'd fallen asleep, missed the actual music, and woken up at the end. Damn! I'd heard that the pianist – it was 'for piano' on this occasion – was really good.

The next time, a couple of years later, I was prepared. I knew what was coming. And I thought I understood it. This Cage chap, what a joker. He's trying to take us for a ride, deliberately provoking us. But it's just a stunt, a hoax – the worst kind of modern art, the kind that scribbles a moustache on the *Mona Lisa* (thank you, Marcel Duchamp) and preserves dead animals in formaldehyde (god bless Damien Hirst).

It was only after I went home and read some reviews that I started to change my mind. As I came to realise – although at the time I had scarcely noticed – the piece wasn't silent at all. Although there was no actual music, no instrument being played, there was an abundance of natural ambient sounds. From outside we might hear traffic noise, rainfall, birdsong, a dog barking, a police siren, the wind, or even thunder. And from inside there would be the usual coughing, sneezing, spluttering and whispering, and the crinkling of sweet wrappers and rustling of programmes.

Cage, I learned, wants us to hear these normal every-day sounds, and he wants us to hear them as music. It's as if he's saying the whole world can be music, if you want it to be. What's more, contrary to my first impression, he isn't mocking classical music or poking fun at concert etiquette. Quite the opposite: he's using this etiquette to his advantage. Assigning a title to a piece, naming the title in a programme, seating an audience in a hall, dimming the lights: aren't these necessary evils? For how else is he to get people to pay attention to the sounds around them – for a full four minutes and 33 seconds?

Blurring the boundaries between noise and music, turning the sounds of life into art, Cage asks us an important question. Not 'What is music?' or 'What is art?' Philosophers have been debating these questions for centuries and we're still none the wiser. He's trying to prompt us to think for ourselves. He's asking us what we want music to be.

Also unsettling our expectations, as well as challenging how we hear, is a piece called *Trio for Springs*, composed a few years later by the musician La Monte Young. The piece begins simply enough: a single note is played by a viola, another by a violin; and then a cello enters with a third and lower note. But the effect is striking, because the notes are long. Loooooooooooooooooooooooooong. When all three instruments play together for the first time, they sustain their notes for no less than one minute and 42 seconds. That's before the cello drops out and the other two instruments continue for a further 40 seconds.

One of Young's disciples, the composer Terry Riley, described his experience of *Trio for Springs* as 'like being on a space station waiting for lunch'. For others, the music recalls the meditative atmosphere of some religious practices.

This idea of meditation strikes a chord with Young himself. In an interview, he described his music's 'sense of time', admitting that it 'has to do with getting away from the earthly sense of direction which goes from birth to death'. He described a phenomenon he called vertical hearing: 'Moving up through the sound of a chord that's sustained, using this to create a drone state of mind.' This mode of hearing, he thought, provided 'a means towards achieving a state of meditation or an altered state of consciousness that can allow you to be more directly in touch with universal structure and a higher sense of order.'

Normally, of course, we attend to music 'horizontally', as a series of events in time. We observe, if only subconsciously, the meandering of melodies, the chattering of rhythms. We follow the way the music ebbs and flows.

Young suggests we try something different, something more akin to the popular psychological concept known as mindfulness – honing in on our experiences in the present moment. According to Young, this present-centred awareness has musical benefits, freeing us to listen and observe with curiosity and openness, rather than with expectations about what's going on. But it also helps us transcend the cut and thrust of daily reality, escape the time-specific routines that structure our lives.

Of course, you can listen to all three of these pieces without knowing any of the background. You don't have to consider the composers' interests and intentions. But you may be missing out not only on the particulars of the individual pieces, but on the basic point of them all. Perhaps you've heard of the phrase 'art about art'? Essentially, it means the art in question is self-reflexive: it takes its own nature and structure, processes and conditions as its primary focus. Sure, it can be newfangled and innovative, breaking with traditions from the past. But what it really likes to do is question, confuse, challenge and obscure its own meaning and purpose, not to mention how it's viewed or heard, watched or listened to.

Modern classical music is no exception. Its purpose is to make us realise that there are different ways to hear music (up or down, vertically or horizontally), different sounds to hear as music (noises from the street, even the coughing of your companion), and different reasons we might not want to bother listening at all.

It reminds us that music is a phenomenon of perception, a creation of our imagination. Anything can be music if we choose to hear it as such. And hearing is not a passive activity for musical couch potatoes. Hearing is an act of composition.

*To stop the flow of music
would be like the stopping
of time itself, incredible
and inconceivable.*
AARON COPLAND

Music on hold

ACCORDING TO EXPERTS at a British think-tank, The New Economics Foundation, the average person spends 45 hours a year on hold on the telephone. According to experts from elsewhere, this is longer than the average person spends having sex.

One of these activities is fun, thrilling and good for the soul. But the other — let's face it — is a pain in the arse. Being on hold means having to wait: for someone you don't know, somewhere you can't imagine, for some unknown length of time. And nobody likes to wait, accustomed as we are to the instant gratifications of modern technology. Furthermore, the technology itself is far from fault-free. Stuck on hold, who hasn't experienced a crackly line, a computer malfunction, even an accidental cut-off? Then there are those annoying voice-overs: 'Your call is important to us'; 'Thank you for your patience. Please continue to hold.' Let's be frank, if your call *were* important and if you *did* have patience, you wouldn't be huffing and puffing with an aching arm.

Classical music, I'm sorry to say, makes this situation worse. I speak here from personal experience, although I'd guess many of you have felt the same. Only last week I was on hold to my bank, waiting for an activation code for an international money transfer. I waited 33 minutes, listening all the while to Antonio Vivaldi's 'Spring', the Violin Concerto in E major from *The Four Seasons*. But 'Spring' doesn't last 33 minutes; it lasts about ten. So I heard the piece three times over and I caught a bit of repetition four.

Not for the first time in my life, and probably not for the last, I succumbed to phone rage. That's the official term for wanting to smash the phone to smithereens, to rant, rave and shout expletives at the disembodied orchestra. It wasn't that I didn't like the music. I love Vivaldi. And I especially love *The Four Seasons*, music that paints pictures so vivid and intense that weather formations always come to mind. But I hate Vivaldi on the phone.

This hatred stems not from any high-minded belief that technology cheapens or devalues the music of the past. What irks me is laziness, unimaginativeness and overkill – the fact that Vivaldi is used to death. You see, when I hear *The Four Seasons* on the phone I don't stop to think, 'I know that piece.' Or 'Isn't that…?' I know I know it. And I know I know I'm going to know it, even before I dial.

As for why Vivaldi is ubiquitous – on the phone, that is – his popularity has much to answer for. Although virtually unknown for about two hundred years, the music of this eighteenth-century Venetian composer (he was also a violinist, impresario, teacher and priest) was successfully revived in the 1940s thanks to a series of prominent performances, recordings, archival studies, editions, festivals and even namesake orchestras. It wasn't long before Vivaldi attained international celebrity, and before his music – particularly his concertos, of which there are several hundred – started to dominate the airwaves.

But there may be more to it than this. Think about Vivaldi's music. It's highly melodic, full of memorable tunes that are easy to hum. The overall mood is casual and sprightly, brisk and upbeat – like an invigorating walk in a gentle breeze. But this mood is unchanging and the melodies repeat; the beat is constant and the metre is invariable; the harmonies are simple and the phrases are regular; and the rhythms chatter endlessly.

According to Robert Fink, professor of music at the University of California, Los Angeles, this uniform and predictable musical quality couldn't be more suited to the on-hold environment. Why? Because this environment itself is designed to be uniform and predictable, radiating an impersonal ambience that regulates emotion and fends off anxiety, minimising the potential for phone rage.

Only now, it seems, we've had enough. We're fed up with Vivaldi.

So what else could we listen to when stuck on the phone? What else would help us pass the time pleasantly? We're bound to have personal preferences. Indeed, as a society we've become increasingly self-selecting, choosing what to watch and when to watch it (witness the MY SKY phenomenon), what to listen to and what to skip (on our iPod, iPad or iPhone).

One solution might be a MY PHONE Shuffle (you heard it here first). This piece of software would let you pick and choose between on-hold tunes. Imagine the possibilities. Waiting on hold, you get sick of Vivaldi so you switch to Maurice Ravel, maybe his *Bolero*. Next you fancy a bit of Gustav Holst, *The Planets*, say. Then some Antonín Dvořák; I'd pick his 'New World' Symphony, No. 9. Perhaps you're even able to access the personal music library you've stored in cyber-space.

If this invention doesn't get off the ground, here are some more suggestions: ten pieces that might work well on the phone, and why.

1 Aaron Copland, *Appalachian Spring* (1944)

When we're stuck on the phone we wish we weren't, and Copland's piece, which began life as a ballet score and ended up winning a Pulitzer Prize, is the ultimate in musical escapism. Capturing the ambience of rural Pennsylvania in the early 1800s, *Appalachian Spring* has become synonymous with pioneer America, its youthful spirit, unbounded possibilities and vast open landscapes. Copland's characteristically 'American' sound – solo woodwind melodies, cavernous supporting strings, slow-to-change basic harmonies, and piercing military-style brass – is everywhere to be heard. Also listen out for the Shaker hymn 'Simple Gifts'. Plucked by the composer from an obscure book of folksongs, it is now one of the most popular American songs.

2 Thomas Tallis, *Spem in alium nunquam habui* (In no other is my hope, circa 1570)

If you're familiar with the clit-lit sensation that is *Fifty Shades of Grey* – and by all accounts some 40 million of us are – you'll have heard of this piece. The novel's handsome hero, S&M enthusiast Christian Grey, enjoys its rich tapestry of sounds, particularly when engaged in his favourite hobby. The richness of the music is easily explained. Tallis uses a 40-voice choir – 40 individual parts, sung by performers arranged in a horseshoe formation – to create a vocal sound of extraordinary intensity and expansiveness. There's some debate over why the composer scored for such a huge choir: one possibility is that the work was written for the 40th birthday of the reigning monarch, Elizabeth I. Whatever the case, and as Mr Grey would likely admit, the music is compelling, as much for the magnitude of its sound as for its carefully interwoven vocal lines.

3 Arnold Schoenberg, *Pelleas and Melisande* (1903)

Any exposure is good exposure, especially for a composer such as Schoenberg, whose name is synonymous with the avant-garde music of the early twentieth century. But Schoenberg also composed some remarkably expressive works, legacies of the so-called Romantic style, with its long-breathed melodies, dramatic outbursts, colourful instrumentation and incantations. *Pelleas and Melisande*, based on a play by Maurice Maeterlinck (the same play that was converted into an opera by Claude Debussy), is one of them. It's classified as a 'symphonic poem', a one-movement piece for symphony orchestra that inspires dramatic or pictorial associations, although without recourse to words, spoken or sung. Pianist Glenn Gould has called it one of the greatest symphonic poems ever written. I'm tempted to agree.

4 Jules Massenet, *Esclarmonde* (1889)

Strange but true, this long-forgotten French opera has a history of being piped down the telephone. When it premiered in Paris in 1889, the city was hosting the Exposition Universelle, an exhibition of the industrial achievements, arts and cultures of countries across the globe. Although the Eiffel Tower, built for the occasion, was the star attraction, visitors also thronged to the Pavillon des Téléphones. Here, seated at specially designated listening stations and kitted out with earphones, men and women could hear live musical performances – transmitted by telephone cables – taking place across the city. *Esclarmonde* was performed one evening and listeners thronged to hear it. One listener, writing for the French daily paper *Le Figaro*, described the strangeness of the experience: 'If one closes one's eyes, one might believe oneself to be in the theatre. A man caught by this illusion puts down his receivers in order to applaud; the laughing of his neighbours brings him back to reality.'

5 Giacomo Puccini, 'Nessun dorma' (None shall sleep, from *Turandot*, 1926)

You might want to sing along.

6 Ennio Morricone, *Once Upon A Time In The West* (director Sergio Leone, 1968)

Who said that film scores were merely background music, secondary to plot, character and visuals? Here's one score that can stand to be apart from the images it so expertly complements. According to some reports, Ennio Morricone composed the music to this classic Western before shooting on the film began, which may explain the score's almost operatic intensity. But what of the sounds themselves? The wailing harmonica, the twanging electric guitar, the clip-clop jauntiness of the banjo, the haunting female intonations: put these together – as Morricone often does – and you have musical riches of the most evocative kind. As 'FatManDoubleZero' tweets: 'When I die and go to heaven, I hope the heavenly orchestra is playing this music at the pearly gates.'

7 Gareth Farr, *Kembang Suling* (Blooming Flute, 1995)

One of the most popular pieces by this much loved New Zealand composer, *Kembang Suling* comprises three movements – to quote Farr, 'three musical snapshots of Asia'. The third, based on traditional South Indian scales, is particularly captivating, with flute acrobatics and a pulsating marimba evoking the vibrancy and charm of exotic lands. It's also a bit of a tease, a musical game of tag. While the marimba repeats a complex rhythmic pattern, the flute tries to play chase, but its imitative melody falls out of sync with that of its keyboard companion. Will the flute ever catch up? Maybe. Maybe not. It'll grab your attention anyhow.

8 Igor Stravinsky, *Étude pour pianola* (Study for Pianola, 1917)

To state the obvious, when we're listening to music on hold our call could be answered at any time. Interruption is guaranteed. So it might make sense to choose an interruptible piece, one that has no obvious structure. Stravinsky's *Étude pour pianola*, which was inspired by music the composer heard on a trip to Madrid, is one such piece. With little sense of direction or forward thrust, the music comprises snatches of melodies, fragmented bass-lines, repeated dance rhythms, ascending runs – all overlapping and competing for attention. The resulting cacophony is not only reminiscent of Madrid's city streets, it's entirely suited to the instrument at hand. The pianola, a self-playing piano fitted with perforated paper rolls, was known for its mechanical, metronomic effects. Stravinsky was quite taken with the instrument, creating new music specifically for it, as well as piano-roll transcriptions of some of his orchestral scores.

9 Karlheinz Stockhausen, *Kontakte* (Contact, 1960)

Like Stravinsky's *Étude*, this piece offers little in the way of momentum or continuity. An early experiment in electronic music, *Kontakte* is best described as a collection of individual sounds – some electronically synthesised, others instrumental – rather than a structured series of musical patterns. Interestingly, the composer described how his approach to the composition allowed him to experiment with space – the ways in which sounds could give the illusion of depth and distance, direction, background and speed. Carefully controlling the volume of the instruments and the reverberation of the electronic sounds, Stockhausen created an artificial space in which his music gallops past the listener, recedes, then gradually emerges again, spins around in circles, shoots up into the stars, explodes like fireworks, and then trickles down to Earth. *Kontakte* – not for the faint-hearted – may well make you feel dizzy. But at least you'll forget how long you've been waiting on the phone.

10 **A Living Composer,** *A New Piece* **(date unknown)**
Well, why not? I can think of several of my students who would jump at the chance to compose on-hold music – to think creatively about how and why certain music works best on the phone. Maybe I'll ask my bank: Can you commission something new? Pleeeeeeeeease?

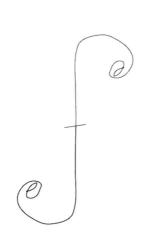

An opera begins long before the curtain goes up and ends long after it has come down. It starts in my imagination, it becomes my life, and it stays part of my life long after I've left the opera house.

MARIA CALLAS

Me, myself
and my music

ONE OF TODAY'S MOST popular apps – a computerised programme that lets you perform tasks on your smartphone or tablet – is a snazzy piece of software called Moodagent. Download it to your hand-held device and it will automatically create playlists of 'songs' from your digital music library, 'song' being internet-speak for music of all kinds. Better still, Moodagent will match these songs to your mood, which you can indicate through touch-sensitive, on-screen buttons labelled 'happy', 'tender', 'sensual' and 'anger'. A press release explains that 'a team of expert musicologists has cracked the emotional codes found in music to create an intelligent system that deciphers every musical property in a song, including moods and emotions'.

Wow, this is impressive! With its 'digital signal processing, artificial intelligence and genuine music science' (hmm?), Moodagent will save us all time – time we might have spent combing through our collections in search of 'songs' that sound good together and suit our mood.

Equally impressive is the fashion industry's latest invention, the 'wearable DJ'. Developed by the Massachusetts Institute of Technology, 'smart clothing' selects music by recognising and responding to the user's emotional temperature, as indicated by physiological signals such as skin conductivity, respiration and muscle tension; these signals are picked up by sensors sewn into the clothing's fabric. According to one report, 485 million of us will be wearing smart clothes by 2018.

These inventions seem truly radical, revolutionising the way we hear music and have it about our person. Moreover, according to market analysts, the new-fangled devices are capitalising on three contemporary consumer trends. First, there's the trend for ubiquitous music: music that's all around us, a sea of sounds we dip in and out of, sometimes paying attention but most often not. Second, there's our preference for personal, private listening. We love the secrecy that comes with earphones and mobile music devices: no one else can enter our musical world and hear what we're hearing. Third, there's our desire for intuitive, mood-matching music. We want music that's both seamlessly integrated into our everyday environment and in sync with our psychological traits.

But hang on a minute. Are these technologies really so radical and these trends really so recent? If you look back over the years you'll find another musical phenomenon, once just as popular, that serves much the same purposes. It's a phenomenon that links music most explicitly with the real physical world, not to mention its living, breathing subjects.

Opera. According to the eighteenth-century Scottish poet Robbie Burns, it's a genre 'where a guy gets stabbed in the back and, instead of dying, he sings'.

Burns is wrong about one thing. Although there's a good deal of dying in opera – from suicide, execution and spousal smothering to the less common death by volcano (in Daniel Auber's *La Muette de Portici*), by poisonous plant (in Léo Delibes' *Lakmé*), and by Jack the Ripper (in Alban Berg's *Lulu*) – it's the women who tend to die, not the men.

But Burns is right about the singing. Everyone sings in opera, no matter what else is going on. Characters may be dying, crying, arguing, hallucinating, dancing, praying or being dragged down to hell: they're still singing all the while.

Song is to opera what dance movement is to ballet and gesture to pantomime. It's the dramatic language of choice, the primary mode of communication. At least so thought Jacopo Peri, an Italian composer and member of the Florence-based Camerata, a group of musicians and intellectuals responsible for the first flowering in the late sixteenth century of what we now know as opera.

In the preface to his second dramatic work *Eurydice*, based on a Greek legend, Peri said he wanted to 'make a simple trial of what the song of our age could do'. Back then there were several types of song, from religious hymns to madrigals, unaccompanied vocal pieces, often with light-hearted or amorous texts, dance-like rhythms and jaunty melodies. Peri and his Camerata colleagues envisaged a new kind of song that would 'imitate a person speaking' while conveying a greater intensity of emotion than was possible through speech alone.

In Peri's operas this new musical speech – we now call it recitative – became the actor-singer's medium of expression. Music was no longer a mere accompaniment to a spoken text, as it was in medieval music theatre. It was designed to convey that text to an audience, to carry the dramatic thread – but without drawing too much attention to itself.

Opera, Peri might have said, is the ultimate ubiquitous music. In the onstage fictional world, music is everywhere, all-encompassing, inescapable. It follows characters around the stage, circling like a school of fish, and continually emanates from their mouths. It's the means through which the stories are told.

In addition, like the ubiquitous music of today — in shopping malls, elevators and restaurants, as well on MP3s and smartphones — music in opera tends not to be heard on a conscious level, at least not by the characters on stage. (The German opera-supremo Richard Wagner once complained that not even audiences paid much attention to opera's music.)

Because it's normal to sing, characters don't stop to wonder why they are conversing in song, or why their singing is being accompanied by an invisible instrumental ensemble. Hence the funny moment towards the end of Gioachino Rossini's 1816 opera *Il Barbiere di Siviglia* (The Barber of Seville).

Count Almaviva and his beloved Rosina, ward of the grumpy Dr Bartolo, are confessing their love for each other inside old Bartolo's home. The barber Figaro, Almaviva's sidekick, is trying to hurry the two along: time is of the essence and they need to escape. They're singing all the time, of course, Figaro mocking the lovers by echoing their sickly sweet phrases. But what's funny is that they continue to sing even when strangers approach. Stopping in their tracks, the three characters sing a full-blown cabaletta — a fast-paced, animated number with several verses and repeats — about the need to 'get out of here quickly'. Surely if the need were that urgent, they would be gone already! It's almost as if Rossini is poking fun at opera's convention of having characters sing. By the time the trio have finished singing, their escape ladder has disappeared. They're trapped.

In opera, music acts like a cocoon, enveloping the characters in a make-believe world where singing is natural and expected. Having said this, there are moments when opera characters do notice music – usually music that's played or sung as an event within the opera's plot. (Music of this kind is called 'diegetic' for it belongs within the 'diegesis', the opera's fictional world.) There are other occasions where it can be difficult to tell. Take, for example, Carmen's opening song in Georges Bizet's 1875 Spanish-themed opera, also set in Seville. As the gypsy girl makes an entrance and sings of the licentious nature of love (you'd recognise the teasing 'Habanera' tune), the audience in the theatre is unsure quite what is going on. Is Carmen in opera mode, singing as is customary? Or is she performing within the plot, flirting in song with the soldiers around her?

Examples such as this remind us of another function of opera music: its ability to create zones or spaces within which a song can take on special meaning. In this example, Carmen blurs these zones: her 'Habanera' is both a public performance for the soldiers and a personal affirmation aimed solely at the audience in the theatre.

Later in the opera the zones become clear. In the mountain wilderness outside Seville, Carmen and her friends Frasquita and Mercedes indulge in a spot of fortune-telling. Carmen's fortune looks ominous: cards foretell her death, as well as that of her on-off lover, the corporal Don José. For the first time in the opera, Carmen's composure begins to crumble. In full view of her friends she sings an aria – an expressive solo number – in contemplation of the destiny awaiting her. Her friends are deaf to this music: they do not hear Carmen's heartfelt words. Nor do they recognise that, also for the first time, Carmen's characteristically exhibitionist and exotic musical style has been replaced by something more conventionally lyrical. This new music, stripped of its gypsy qualities, is inaudible to the characters onstage. It erects invisible walls around the heroine, creating a theatrical space in which Carmen, alone, can reflect on her fate.

Musical spaces like this are essential to opera. Like Shakespearean monologues, they allow characters moments of privacy, creating a secret theatre that no one else can enter and no one else can hear.

It's easy enough to draw an analogy with the secret theatres of today, the ones created by mobile music gadgets chanelling sound through headphones. How often do you see someone walking down a street, plugged into the latest technology, head bopping, lips miming, hands motioning – all to a seemingly silent soundtrack?

Clearly, you have no clue as to the music in question; you're not in the same headspace as the other person. You may as well be Frasquita or Mercedes during Carmen's mountain meltdown, oblivious to what's going on.

Opera relies on these secret moments, not only to provide a dramatic pause and an opportunity for a character to reflect, but to match music to mood. Let's look at a passage from George Handel's *Samson*, a sacred drama that premiered at Covent Garden, London, in 1743. Incidentally, this was a time when Handel, a composer of German origin, was enthusiastically embraced by the British, and when opera itself was enormously popular across Europe, attracting audiences of aristocrats and noble families, political figureheads and commoners.

The passage is another aria, and like most arias it represents a dramatic pause: nothing much happens to move the plot forward.

Samson, a slave to the Philistines, is in contemplative mode. Surrounded by a chorus of Israelites, he laments his loss of sight:

Total eclipse! no sun, no moon,

All dark amidst the blaze of noon!

O glorious light! no cheering ray,

To glad my eyes with welcome day!

Why thus depriv'd Thy prime decree?

Sun, moon and stars are dark to me!

This 'darkness' – both literal, Samson's blindness, and metaphorical, his despair – is carefully depicted by Handel. The music is slow-paced and in the key of E minor. (Minor keys are often associated with sadness and melancholy.) And it's full of descending motifs. The first, played in unison by the strings, actually sounds more like the end of a phrase – a musical full stop – than the start of one. Is the aria over before it's even begun?

When the voice does enter, the strings fall silent. Unaccompanied, Samson is vulnerable and alone. There's no sun, no moon and no musical beat to follow, no chordal accompaniment, no cushion of strings.

The gloominess is oppressive. If you take a closer look at the score, you'll see that even the structure of the aria has a dramatic role. Handel's arias are normally in three sections, the third being a repetition of the first, often embellished by the singer. But here the third section is cut drastically short.

All these musical effects serve the same purpose: to make the audience aware that Samson has vegetated into a state of complete hopelessness. Instead of determining the music's course, he seems to be drowning in it – in a score that is saturated with musical signs of closure. What we hear may offer insight into the mind of a character, but it's also testimony to music's power over the emotions, which Handel and his contemporaries referred to as 'affects'.

A different impression arises from a monologue in

Act II of Modest Mussorsgky's 1869 historical opera *Boris Godunov*. Boris, the tsar of Russia (from 1598 to 1605), begins in a calm and sober frame of mind, describing his years of reign and his frustrated good intentions. But he quickly becomes agitated at the thought of the child-prince Dmitry, of whose death he stands accused.

Mussorsgky is an expert psychological profiler: the music follows every twist and turn in Boris's thoughts. Melodies pop up in the orchestra to remind us of people and events, both past and present. Moreover, as the tsar reaches breaking point his music does too: the opening vocal melody, stately and noble, disintegrates into a chaos of note-values, rests and random pitches.

This moment-by-moment mirroring of music and emotion – something Mussorsgky toned down in a revised version of the opera – is quite unlike Handel's manner of musical characterisation. The German composer is no psychologist: his music is not based on the analytical observation of mental processes. Instead, he seeks to stylise in music a single 'affect' – a lingering moment of heightened emotion.

Mussorsgky, in contrast, aims for accuracy in psychological expression. Inspired by the scientific revelations of his day, especially the evolutionary theories of Charles Darwin, he considered music to be a kind of laboratory experiment into human thought and behaviour. As a result, his music can be wild and unpredictable, impulsive and erratic – just like human beings ourselves. In the monologue described it is strikingly intense, brutally upfront: you could call it an accurate depiction of a mind continually churning.

Current thinking may have you believe that opera is ridiculous, outdated and irrelevant, a waste of both your time and your money. And there's no denying it: opera is expensive, both to go to and to stage. And when you attend you do need to suspend disbelief and accept the convention of continuous song. But you might well ask: Is there a genre more firmly entrenched in the world, one with more obvious human priorities, not to mention a more psychologically motivated musical accompaniment? Opera is bang on trend. Like today's mobile music players, it creates an environment in which music can be everywhere, secret, and in sync with emotions.

Moreover, opera is manipulating these trends in a way that the newfangled gadgets are not – not yet anyway. Recent operas – yes, there are a few examples, although admittedly not many – regularly exploit the ubiquity of music. Think of Karlheinz Stockhausen's 29-hour opera cycle *Licht* (Light, subtitled 'The Seven Days of the Week'), composed between 1977 and 2003. As well as the usual singing and orchestral accompaniment, the opera's music escapes from the stage into speakers around the auditorium, the theatre foyer and even the skies outside. *Mittwoch* (Wednesday, staged for the first time in 2012) features the now infamous 'Helicopter String Quartet'. Four musicians are carried into the air, each in their own helicopter, playing their instruments over the noise of whirring blades.

As for private spaces and mood music, both are carefully created, then blown to smithereens, in John Adams' 2005 opera *Doctor Atomic*, which is about the countdown and testing of the first atomic bomb. While the bomb itself is identified by clockwork rhythms and the ethereal sound of harp and glockenspiel, intended to symbolise the mysterious properties of plutonium, the anxiety of those who await the explosion also has a distinctive profile, associated with music that recalls the sumptuous styles of Wagner and Debussy.

This psychological realm explodes with the bomb itself. Pulsating chords gain rhythmic momentum, a chorus sings a strangely beautiful ode, everything seems to get quicker and louder, and then... electronic noise and sound effects. The crying of a child. The murmuring of a crowd. And the disembodied voice of a Japanese woman asking for water, asking where her husband might be.

Merging his carefully conceived sound worlds, Adams links the stage goings-on and the characters' anxiety with the reality of 'Little Boy' and 'Fat Man', the bombs that dropped from the sky in August 1945. This allusion to the events at Hiroshima and Nagasaki, events that Doctor Atomic sets in motion, is a trenchant reminder of the horror and destruction that shattered daily lives. It reminds us, too, of opera's power to convey such devastating events.

The artist must forget the audience, forget the critics, forget the technique, forget everything but love for the music. Then, the music speaks through the performance, and the performer and the listener will walk together with the soul of the composer, and with God.

MSTISLAV ROSTROPOVICH

Performance
anxiety

WHY CAN'T MUSIC be rid of performers? Why can't orchestras abandon their instruments? Why can't singers simply vanish from the stage? In 1920 the American composer Charles Ives (he was also an insurance executive) asked something similar: 'Why can't music go out in the same way it comes in to a man, without having to crawl over a fence of sounds, thoraxes, catguts, wire, wood and brass?'

These questions may seem ridiculous. Indeed, ask them to a class of fresh-faced students, as I did recently, and their faces will wrinkle and frown.

'Music without performers?' one student said, clearly incredulous.

'Without instruments?' said an unbelieving other. 'Without people having to press keys or pluck strings, or make any other kind of movement?'

'Duh,' came a voice from the back of the room. 'That's impossible. That's like poetry without words, or, hmm, drama without characters. It just can't exist.'

Ives thought it could. An amateur composer for much of his life, he believed he could separate himself from the world of practical music-making and compose simply for his own amusement, without performance in mind. According to some sources, Ives rarely heard his music being performed and didn't much care whether it was or wasn't. Attracted by the philosophical notion of transcendentalism, a somewhat mystical belief in our ability to transcend the drudgery of day-to-day life and achieve spiritual oneness with nature, he regarded music less as a real-life activity than as an imaginary ideal or concept. As for performers, well in Ives's transcendental world view they didn't have much of a role to play.

Unbeknown to many (at least to many of my students), the status or function of performers has long been questioned. At the turn of the sixth century, the Roman philosopher Boethius described performers as slaves, equating technical skill with manual labour. Centuries later, in the age of J.S. Bach, performers were respected for the very craftsmanship that Boethius had scorned, although some – freelance musicians known as 'beer fiddlers' (they performed in return for alcohol, as well as bread and cheese) – were ridiculed as drunken beggars. In the nineteenth century, the pianist and composer Franz Liszt rose to fame as a travelling virtuoso, dazzling audiences across Europe with his technical precision and emotional abandon. Yet this didn't stop critics complaining. They fired insults at Liszt's over-the-top interpretations and theatrical manner of performance – the physical excesses of which tortured both his instrument and his audience.

In Ives' time this debate came to a head. Composers questioned not only the strengths and weaknesses of individual performers, but the necessity of performance itself. Italian composer Ferrucio Busoni, himself an acclaimed pianist, suggested that 'the musical work of art exists whole and intact before it has sounded and after the sound has finished'. Arnold Schoenberg, the Austrian composer known for his avant-garde music, seemed to agree: he argued that 'a musical work doesn't have to live – that is, be performed, at all costs'. Writing about his 1936 violin concerto, Schoenberg famously declared, 'I am delighted to add another unplayable work to the repertoire. I want the concerto to be difficult and I want the little finger to become longer.'

What arrogance! What contempt! It's easy to get exasperated and shake our fists at this lack of concern on composers' parts for the performance of their music. But perhaps we should remember the possible reasons performers were essentially demoted in the early twentieth century. I suspect these reasons had something to do with the general intellectual outlook of the time. Modernist thought, and modernism in general, promoted the idea that a work of art could speak for itself. The work's meaning and significance lay in its internal qualities and technical innovations, rather than in its social function and expressive qualities.

Considered like this, a composer's score was a stream of scribbled notes that contained everything of value about a piece, and everything that could be understood by an objective observer. Performers were regarded as mere machines: their job was to transmit the composer's score as accurately as possible, without exercising any creative judgement of their own.

Perhaps we should also remember how far we've come. If a general disregard for performance seems to have characterised the early twentieth century, the opposite marks the early twenty-first. In the last few years, performers have become more and more central to the world of classical music. There are the celebrity types, a breed that began in the 1990s with The Three Tenors and has since spawned the singers Andrea Bocelli and Katherine Jenkins, the violinist André Rieu, and groups such as Il Divo, The Irish Tenors and The Ten Tenors. Love them or hate them, these glamorous glossy-haired musical idols have done much to promote the classical repertoire. Or at least parts of it. Rieu is renowned for his Viennese waltzes, while Jenkins prefers well-known operatic numbers, plus traditional folk songs and carols. And all indulge in classical crossovers, covering popular hits by the likes of Frank Sinatra and Céline Dion.

But there are other performers, less hyped up and commercially packaged, who have made greater strides to invigorate the classics and help us hear them anew.

Jane Chapman

Described by London's *Metro* newspaper as 'the hippest harpsichordist around', Chapman is almost single-handedly responsible for the revival of an instrument long thought dead and buried. The keyboard of choice for two hundred years, the harpsichord was gradually eclipsed in the late eighteenth century by the fortepiano, the instrument for which Haydn and Mozart composed.

Unearthing a treasure trove of little-known music, Chapman has brought back to life her instrument and its antiquated sound – delicate, elegant and restrained, with a clipped quality that contrasts strongly with the resonance and richness of the piano. Listen to one of her recordings and this sound will transport you back to a time when the instrument, often lavishly decorated inside and out, was the plaything and furniture piece of the European aristocracy.

But Chapman has another talent. Keen to keep up with the latest musical developments, she has commissioned and collaborated on some modern classical works. Several of these attempt to transform the harpsichord's sound, calling for Chapman to experiment with different performance techniques: stroking and plucking the harpsichord's strings from inside (yes, inside) the instrument; using an electric bow to make the strings vibrate continuously; and even removing the strings entirely. (If you're curious, listen to her version of György Ligeti's *Continuum*.)

Chapman professes to love this kind of radical experimentation. The harpsichord, she told *The Wall Street Journal*, is a kind of magic box: open its lid and you'll unleash a torrent of sounds and effects.

Patrick Gallois

I've been in love with this French flutist since I heard his recording of Mozart's two concertos for flute, composed in the late 1770s. A flutist myself, I have heard countless versions of these pieces, both repertoire staples: nothing much else was written for the flute between about 1750 and 1900. And I've noticed a general trend among performers: overindulgence. Imagine hordes of James Galway wannabes, gold flutes and all, playing Mozart as if it were Puccini – with too much vibrato ('wobble') to the sound, too much rubato (speeding up and slowing down), and a general gushiness that obscures the original character of the pieces. As Mozart envisaged them, these concertos were animated conversations between flute and orchestra. (The word concerto, from the Latin *concertare* – meaning both to contend with and to agree with – implies a dramatic dialogue.) However, most flutists ramp up the drama. Over-miked, they turn a light-hearted exchange into a heated soliloquy.

But not Patrick. He's not inclined to wallow or swoon. And he's not afraid to withdraw from the spotlight, quietening down when the orchestra has the tune. With Gallois and company the musical dialogue is nicely balanced, not to mention characterful: listening to Gallois' recording I find myself imagining the stock-in-trade characters of comic opera, a genre in which Mozart excelled. Opera buffa, as it was known, was a type of breezy, happy-ending opera that rose to popularity – first in Italy and then across Europe – in the eighteenth century. Servants and masters, village folk and noble-men, star-crossed lovers, blundering fools and cunning tricksters: many of these come to mind as Gallois and his orchestra engage in their playful, good-natured antics.

The Monteverdi Choir and English Baroque Soloists
Like Gallois, these two groups, both directed by English conductor John Eliot Gardiner, are known for their attempts to recreate the musical styles and idioms of a composer's own period. Under Gardiner, this calls for serious prep. Historical evidence is consulted, manu-scripts unearthed, old instruments restored, instrumental techniques resurrected. It can also call for physical

pilgrimage. At the new millennium, to mark the 250th anniversary of J.S. Bach's death, Gardiner and his musicians began a 12-month odyssey through 14 European countries and the United States, intent on performing all 198 of Bach's surviving sacred cantatas – vocal compositions in several movements – in churches, monasteries and priories, some of which had special associations with Bach himself.

Even more specifically, Gardiner wanted to perform Bach's cantatas on, or as close as possible to, the Sunday or religious feast day for which they were initially composed. For New Year's Day 2000 he programmed 'Jesu, nun sei gepreiset' (Jesus, now be praised), which had originally been performed on January 1, 1725. And on April 29, 2000 he conducted 'Halt im Gedächtnis Jesum Christ' (Hold in remembrance Jesus Christ), written by Bach for Quasimodogeniti, the first Sunday after Easter.

This was no small undertaking, especially as all the performances were recorded by the conductor's own label, Soli Deo Gloria (To the Glory of God Alone, the words inscribed by Bach on his cantata scores) after the big shots at Deutsche Grammophon pulled out.

If you can get your hands on one of these CDs, I bet your ears will prick. First, there are the singers. Buoyant, agile and sprightly, the choir conveys the dance-like verve so essential to Bach's music, yet so often overlooked. Second, there's the ensemble: hollow-sounding flutes; raucous, chirpy oboes; sparkling trumpets pitched very high; light and crisp violins; lilting lower strings; and rapid-fire, sharply articulated drums. These instruments, which sound so different from those of today's orchestras, are either eighteenth-century originals or copies, and each has a specific sound quality. You'll hear how they pierce through the ensemble, resulting in the kaleidoscopic sound associated with 'period' performance.

So why not pretend you're a part of the pilgrimage – better still, part of Bach's original congregation – and hear the cantatas as the composer intended them, or as close as we can ever get to that unknown.

Ad Hoc

The name says it all: spontaneous, inventive, off-the-cuff. This little-known instrumental ensemble, based in Rochester, New York, is quietly changing the face of classical performance. How? Well, the answer has nothing to do with the music the group chooses to perform. And neither is it a matter of performance technique or musical style. What's unique about Ad Hoc is its attitude to performance, its sense of how classical music might best communicate with its audience.

Ad Hoc treats performances more like jams than concerts. Listeners can wander in and out, dress informally and munch on nibbles. The ensemble has no official home, no dress code and no fixed membership: people come and go, so the line-up changes for each performance. So does the musical programme – that's when it's even announced. Free 'Chalkboard Concerts' – inspired by cafes' chalkboard menus with their daily specials and lists of fresh produce – name the music to be performed right at the last minute. Only when you turn up do you find out what's in store.

The group also offers open rehearsals and sight-reading parties, opportunities for the public to see how music is made and how an ensemble comes together (often at short notice, with little time to practise and little in the way of funds). This rare insider access is a real treat, especially for young people and budding amateurs. More than this, though, it's a sharp reminder of the illusion the classical recording industry seeks to promote – the illusion of the impeccably polished, acoustically flawless and seemingly effortless performance, the one we rave about, compare all others to, and store in our memories and/or our digital music libraries. This illusion is, of course, precisely that. In reality, performance has nervous excitement, sweaty palms and racing hearts, anxious looks and orgasmic tingles – things recording cannot capture. Thankfully Ad Hoc can.

Los Reciclados (The Recycled Orchestra)

So too can the ensemble known as Los Reciclados, if its members, the underprivileged children of Cateura, Paraguay, are to be believed. Interviewed for the documentary film *Landfill Harmonic* (check out the trailer on YouTube), a young girl called Ada Maribel describes 'a feeling of butterflies in my stomach … a feeling I don't know how to explain'. It's a feeling she gets when she plays her violin. But Ada's is not your normal learner instrument. Nor is it an eighteenth-century replica or a 1667 Stradivarius (as owned by Mr Rieu). This violin is a piece of scrap, made from recycled material from one of Cateura's landfills.

Los Reciclados, conducted by local man Favio Chavez, makes classical music out of trash — 1,500 tonnes of which, according to a UNICEF report, is dumped on the slums of Cateura each day. Cellos, trumpets, flutes, percussion — all were once oil cans, food tins, furniture, even cooking implements. Yet all are now treasured possessions, instruments giving joy and meaning to the lives of one of the most downtrodden of South American communities. 'My life would be worthless without music,' says another young girl on the documentary, as Mozart's *Eine Kleine Nachtmusik* is played by her friends in the orchestra, and images of rubbish bags being piled up and then rummaged through flash before our eyes.

I'm reminded of Ives and Schoenberg and the rest of the anti-performance brigade. A century ago the meaning of music may well have been thought to reside within the composer's score, the much revered manuscript. Today, for the community of Cateura, this meaning is found in performance, in participation, in the garbage that's thrown out, knocked together and cradled in children's arms.

Every work of art is an uncommitted crime.

THEODOR ADORNO

Interventions

TEAM BRITNEY HAS STAGED several, attempting to force the troubled singer into therapy. President Obama has ruled over his fair share, putting military or economic pressure on nations that don't fall in line. And now artists are engaged in them too – interventions, deliberate attempts to change or coerce a person, group or thing.

Wikipedia describes an artistic intervention as an interaction with a previously existing artwork that disturbs the work in some way and flaunts the expectations of its audience. For example, at 'Flip', a 2004 art exhibition in Cape Town, South Africa, a collection of seventeenth-century Dutch paintings was hung facing the walls of the gallery, not the onlookers. That same year, an Italian art student wrapped a well-known equestrian statue on a busy road in West London in almost 80 rolls of bright red duct tape. And let's not forget what happened two years later at a popular Paris show, where a 77-year-old Frenchman took a hammer to Marcel Duchamp's *Fountain*, a porcelain urinal once voted the most influential artwork of the twentieth century.

Wacky, outrageous and provocative, these incidents upend our assumptions about the status of art, and raise questions about the distinction between creativity and vandalism. A case in point: whereas the duct-tape devotee, Eleonora Aguiari, was applauded for her ingenuity, the hammering Frenchman, Pierre Pinoncelli, was arrested on grounds of sabotage.

But all of these examples concern visual art. What about classical music? Have people 'intervened' with this too?

So far in this book I've talked about changes to classical music's traditional contexts — using classical pieces on the phone, revamping the concert hall dynamic, encouraging audience interaction. And there are many similar examples. In New York, a barge moored under Brooklyn Bridge acts as a floating concert hall. In London, the respected Orchestra of the Age of the Enlightenment performs 'late-night and laid-back' in nightclub settings. In Tokyo, audiences at 'Sleepy Bed

Concerts' are provided with cushions, duvets and gallons of Häagen-Dazs ice cream.

But these interventions only scrape the surface. What about interfering with the music itself, the actual notes written by composers? If one of the accusations against classical music is that it is staid, self-absorbed and backwards-looking — in the words of the *New Yorker* critic Alex Ross, focused on 'the manic polishing of a display of masterpieces' — then chipping away at these masterpieces may present another way forward.

Paul Whitty, a composer on the fringe of the classical music establishment and a former colleague of mine, is a keen interventionist. His music not only turns up in the strangest of places, from a traffic interchange to a fridge-freezer compartment, it also does the strangest of things to classical pieces we all know and cherish.

Take Whitty's 2007 work *Thirty-Nine Pages*, an 'intervention' on the much-loved Sonata for Violin and Piano by Belgian composer César Franck. Written in 1886 and offered as a wedding gift to the violinist Eugène Ysaÿe, Franck's sonata is typically Romantic. This means it's heart-on-the-sleeve stuff, full of soaring melodies, long-winded phrases and frequent changes of mood. (A more intellectual definition might be that the sonata dates from a period in Western history when music and the other arts turned away from the guiding principles of the eighteenth-century Enlightenment —

thought, reason, rationalism and uniformity – and, partly in response to the increasing industrialisation of nineteenth-century society, began to cultivate an intensely emotional mode of expression.)

Franck's sonata is based on a small set of themes that recur throughout – we call this 'cyclic form' – and the overall structure is loose and rhapsodic. Because of this, the music sounds spontaneous (the technical term is 'improvisatory'), like an off-the-cuff dialogue between two instruments, treated more as equals than as solo violin with piano accompaniment.

It's also highly poetic and almost feverish. A dramatic urgency propels the music towards one climax after another. No surprise, then, that the sonata has long captivated audiences. Back in the day, the French composer Vincent d'Indy, a pupil of Franck, described it as 'a musical monument', foreseeing the popularity that would ensue. In the 1950s one of Franck's biographers, a French writer called Léon Vallas, described the 'spiritual' and 'elevated' music as 'a sort of poetry of religion'. More recently, the Grammy-award-winning violinist Joshua Bell has spoken of the sonata as a masterpiece and acclaimed its 'nuance, sensuality and transcendent beauty'.

All this, it seems, is lost on Whitty. In *Thirty-Nine Pages*, he takes this most lyrical and impassioned of all sonatas and bleaches it entirely of emotion. He starts by fragmenting the sonata, not into the customary four movements but into pages – all 39 pages of the published score. Next, from these 39 pages he derives 38 short 'episodes', each of which relates to a particular page or two. One episode relates to all 39 pages.

It's difficult, at least on first hearing, to make out much of Franck's original music, since Whitty operates on the smallest of small scales and with almost scientific scrutiny. Having isolated individual pitches, rhythms and chords, he repeats them over and over, or else rearranges them into new and unfamiliar patterns.

To give you a taste, one of Whitty's episodes features only the note A – but all the As that appear on one of Franck's 39 pages, whether high-pitched or low, loud or quiet, harshly accented or feather light. In another episode, he reorganises the sequence of notes on a page, creating a descending chromatic scale from Franck's intricate tapestry of melodies.

Whitty calls this 'deconstruction', a highfalutin word to describe this radical re-jigging of another artist's work. Others have compared his method to an archaeological dig. They imagine the composer in desert sands, excavating Franck's score for its basic raw materials, 'uncovering precious artefacts millimetre by millimetre', in the words of Catherine Nelson, a reviewer for string music magazine *The Strad*.

Tim Rutherford-Johnson, another music critic, offers a more domestic description. Whitty's *Pages*, he says, has the look of 'a bed after the sleeper has awoken and left:

a partial imprint, a scent, perhaps a hair on the pillow. ... It's not enough to reconstruct the person, but you can tell that someone has been there.'

I like this analogy. It captures what seem to be the two contrasting ideas underpinning Whitty's *Pages*: randomness and precision. Leaving a hair on a pillow is accidental and unplanned, not the result of a conscious decision. Likewise, Whitty's music seems to have been composed at random. From the pitches isolated – all those A notes, for example – to the fact the episodes can be played in any order, much about *Thirty-Nine Pages* seems fortuitous. Yet much is also precise. One hair, one pitch, one page at a time, the music gives clues to a shadowy presence lurking somewhere within.

What is Whitty hoping to achieve? The conservatives among us may say he's just messing with Franck's music for the hell of it, doing more harm than good. But what if it's the exact opposite? What if you find hearing Whitty's *Pages* a refreshing, exciting and even startling experience, a bit like meeting the newborn child of an old friend? You may not recognise the child at first glance, may not immediately spot the similarities between parent and offspring, but then you see a facial expression, a pose, a mannerism of some sort, and you're reminded of your friend; you're reminded that he or she lives on in this new physical form.

Moreover, besides their similar genetic makeup, parent and offspring can reveal a lot about one another, a lot that old friends may find surprising. It's the same with Franck and Whitty. *Thirty-Nine Pages* may seem at first like an awkward, unconventional child, but give it time and it will show you things about Franck's sonata that you may otherwise overlook.

For instance, I'd challenge anyone listening to Whitty's episodes not to notice the poise, precision and energy – the sheer effort and discipline – that go into every stroke of the bow, every compression of the piano's keys. These, the rigours of musical performance, are often lost on listeners. Whitty brings them to our attention. He forces us to recognise that each note, each rhythm, each repeated pattern is a manufactured and man-made phenomenon, the result of conscious physical exertion and tutored mental alertness.

He also forces us to recognise the specific qualities of individual sounds. Listening to all those A notes, for example, I hear some that are pot-bellied and swollen, bulging in the middle before fading into oblivion. Others are like pin pricks, lightweight and barely there. No sooner do you hear them than they vanish into silence. Several more are loud and long-lasting. They make me think of darts shooting through the air, their flight path focused and straight, their end unexpected and abrupt.

Clearly, Whitty is playing with our imagination. He's encouraging us to hear sounds in new ways. But he's also playing with something else – our memory of Franck's sonata. Disassembling the music, breaking it up into bits and pieces and then randomly rearranging the rubble, he is asking which bits we recognise and which bits we don't, which bits sound familiar, sound like Franck, and which don't. He's basically asking us about the sonata's identity – what we consider to be its essential components.

These are deep and difficult questions because, when you stop to think about it, what exactly *is* César Franck's Sonata for Violin and Piano? What does it take to *be* – and *be remembered as* that piece? Is the sonata more than the sum of its parts? Or can a single fragment – say, half a melody or a particular chord – serve to identify it in our minds?

Thirty-Nine Pages may well deconstruct Franck's sonata, as Whitty says, but it also deconstructs the whole business of hearing. For the answers to these complex philosophical questions depend on – well, they depend on the title of this book, on how we hear classical music, how we perceive, identify, recognise and remember the age-old pieces we love.

I shouldn't end without mentioning some other musical interventions. There has been quite a flush of them in the last few decades, something critics see as a sign of the diversity and eclecticism of contemporary musical culture. Arvo Pärt's *Credo* (1968), Luciano Berio's *Sinfonia* (1969), Michael Nyman's *In Re Don Giovanni* (1977), Laurie Anderson's 'O Superman (For Massenet)'

(1981), John Cage's *Europeras* 1 and 2 (1987) and John Oswald's *Plunderphonics* (1989) are just some examples. All 'intervene' on classical music, and more often than not on famous pieces.

But they are not the only cases. If you turn back the clock you'll find an embarrassment of riches.

In 1962, the Czech composer Jan Klusák penned his *Variations on a Theme by Gustave Mahler* – according to one report 'what Mahler would have written if he were Klusák'. However, 67 years earlier Mahler himself had engaged in a spot of retouching, changing the orchestration of symphonies by Beethoven and Robert Schumann.

In the late nineteenth century, Ferrucio Busoni began what would be a lifelong love affair with J.S. Bach. He prepared new editions of Bach's music for publication and performance, new arrangements for modern instruments, and new compositions based on Bach's melodies. Perhaps he had learnt from the master himself, for back in the eighteenth century Bach had been known to fiddle, either with his own music – he apparently revised and recycled several compositions – or with the music of Vivaldi, whose violin concertos he famously arranged for keyboard.

Music historians have long debated the hows and whys of interventions. They worry over the difference between quotation, allusion, adaptation, arrangement, variation, pastiche and simple borrowing, not to mention the legitimacy or 'correctness' of each case. But they agree on the implications for listeners. Hearing a musical intervention, we hear music history brought back to life. We listen in on a conversation between one composer and another, sensing how lines of influence unravel and unwind.

You may say that this historical aspect is common to all classical music. Composers, even the most modern and innovative, tend to build their music from pre-existing styles, engaged in a constant conversation with the past. However, the pieces I've just mentioned bring this conversation to the fore. They ask us to 'intervene' ourselves, to actively participate in the dialogue.

Remember Whitty's *Pages*, how the composer calls on our knowledge and experience, activating our memory of Franck's piece in order to elicit our response? Hearing Whitty's odd-sounding episodes we're encouraged to think for ourselves – to make connections, assimilate styles, and imagine ways in which one sound, one page, one piece may relate to another.

For me, this is a liberating experience: my mind is free to wander, to recall musical encounters I've had in the past while envisaging new ones I may have in the future.

'Experience' seems a good word to use. *Thirty-Nine Pages* should be understood not as a musical work or a musical piece, or even a musical composition. These terms imply something finished and fixed that exists apart from its listeners. But in order to live, *Pages* needs listeners. It needs us to untangle the knotty relationships between composers past and present.

There are two means of
refuge from the miseries
of life: music and cats.
ALBERT SCHWEITZER

The happiness project

YOU DON'T HAVE TO look far, in this day and age, to find someone or something in trouble. The media chatter endlessly about social strife and tightening belts. Television indulges in prime-time torture, seeming to celebrate nightmare scenarios (*Air Crash Investigation*, *Motorway Patrol*) and disaster-prone heroes (Rick from *The Walking Dead*, Patrick Jane from *The Mentalist*). Books can be especially agonising. Spend ten minutes in a library and you'll discover a din of misery, from no-nonsense explanations of the economy (*Meltdown*, *And Then The Roof Caved In*), to political diatribe (*Culture of Corruption*), environmental crusade (*Dire Predictions*) and wrong-footed self-help (*This Is Why You're Fat*).

Could this book turn the tide? Can hearing classical music bring hope and happiness?

There's good news from the United States. According to researchers in Florida, a daily dose of classical music can reduce chronic osteoarthritic pain in elderly patients. A team from Michigan State University has reported that the classical repertoire – as well as 'classical jazz' and 'new age' music – can increase blood levels of inter-leukin-1, an immune-boosting protein that protects against viruses and cancers. At Stanford University, scientists have shown that musical training can help children with learning disabilities read and process spoken language more efficiently. And over at the Duke Cancer Center in North Carolina, medical practitioners have used classical pieces to help reduce anxiety in patients undergoing prostate biopsies.

Attempting not only to quantify but to explain the effects of music is Mark Tramo, a musician, composer and scientist at the Harvard Medical School. Using various brain-imaging techniques, Tramo observes which bits of the brain are active when we listen to music, which bits carry information about melody, harmony and rhythm, and which bits affect how we think and feel. Discussing his findings on the American television series *Closer to Truth*, Tramo said, 'Music taps into so many different aspects of cognitive as well as emotional processing that it would be hard to believe it wouldn't have some sort of a positive effect.'

This is all very exciting. Classical music, it seems, can help spread pleasure and joy. It can be a learning aid and a pacifier, a means of pain relief and disease prevention. It can even work its magic on Friesian cattle. According to psychologists at the University of Leicester, cows that are exposed to Beethoven's 'Pastoral' Symphony produce more milk than those cooped up in silent cowsheds.

But there may be more to it than this. Classical music isn't all sugary sweet and easy on the ears. Listen to the epilogue of Symphony No. 6 by the English composer Ralph Vaughan-Williams. 'Every drop of blood seemed frozen in one's veins,' said the musician and broadcaster Deryck Cooke, who attended the London premiere on April 21, 1948. And yes, it is truly frightening music, a quiet eerie wasteland in which a single melody, repeated over and over, wanders aimlessly.

Classical composers are not all happiness gurus. Indeed, many have been quite disturbed. Anton Bruckner had a morbid fascination with dead bodies (some say he was a necrophiliac) and also suffered from obsessive compulsive disorder. Hector Berlioz, a tormented soul, set out to kill his former fiancée, along with her mother and her intended husband – although luckily for them he thought better of it.

And there are other disconcerting facts – about composers' racist views (Pyotr Ilyich Tchaikovsky, Richard

Wagner), deep-seated misogyny (Charles Ives), chauvinistic xenophobia (Camille Saint-Saëns), casual homophobia (Igor Stravinsky), and general bigotry (the Australian Percy Grainger, also a flagellomaniac with a mother fixation).

With these facts in mind, I wonder whether the aforementioned scientific research will unwittingly sell classical music short, branding it as a medicinal pick-me-up, a stress-reducer, a fluffy pillow. Sure, classical pieces can make us feel joy and tenderness, but they can also induce more nuanced emotional responses.

In his 1859 novel *Home of the Gentry*, the Russian author Ivan Turgenev described one man's complex response to a piece for classical piano:

> The sweet, passionate melody captivated his heart from the first note; it was full of radiance, full of the tender throbbing of inspiration and happiness and beauty, continually growing and melting away; it rumoured of everything on Earth that is dear and secret and sacred to mankind; it breathed of immortal sadness and it departed from the Earth to die in the heavens.

Just four years earlier, in an essay on Berlioz's 'Harold' Symphony, the pianist and composer Franz Liszt described a similar marriage of happiness and sadness, 'pure sorrow' and 'pure joy', 'complete relaxation' and 'positive energy', 'extreme satisfaction' and 'absolute despair'. For Liszt, classical music evoked the entire

gamut of human emotions: 'the shadings and modula-
tions of feeling', the 'gradual transitions' between contrasting moods. It plumbed the depths of the human soul,
he said, shining a torchlight on to thoughts and feelings
that might otherwise remain concealed.

Once, towards the end of a production of Puccini's
1904 opera *Madame Butterfly*, I saw an old woman cry.
Too young then to fully appreciate the dramatic events
in this most tragic of love stories, I had no idea why she
was crying or what was making her so sad. The music I
heard sounded beautiful and luscious. And incredibly
loud: I was amazed by the sheer volume of sound
emanating from the dainty singer on the stage. Where
was her microphone? I thought to myself.

The woman dabbing her eyes must have heard
something different: perhaps music that laid bare the
naïve devotion of a young Japanese woman scorned by
an unscrupulous American man; perhaps music that
bespoke the man's innate racism and boorish behaviour;
or perhaps, as opera experts would have us believe, music
that illustrated the stock-in-trade convention of how a
tragic opera heroine must sound before suicide – lyrical,
ravishing and thoroughly European.

Attending the opera wasn't an entirely happy experience for me or for the sad woman. But it was an intense
imaginative encounter: we were both in thrall to the
music. A sea of possibility raged before us, a myriad of
ways to hear, to think and to feel. And we jumped right in.

Books and recordings

First, the books I've enjoyed and been inspired by:

Big Bangs: The Story of Five Discoveries that Changed Musical History, Howard Goodall: Vintage, 2011
A lively account of the moments that made music what it is today; intelligent and fun to read.

But Is It Art?, Cynthia Freeland: Oxford University Press, 2001
A small book that tackles big questions about the meaning and significance of art.

The Danger of Music and Other Anti-Utopian Essays, Richard Taruskin: University of California Press, 2009
A collection of press articles and essays by one of the

towering music writers of our time, known for his hard-hitting, no-nonsense approach.

Douglas Lilburn: His Life and Music, Philip Norman: Canterbury University Press, 2006
The one and only biography.

First Nights: Five Musical Premieres, Thomas Forrest Kelly: Yale University Press, 2001
Kelly recreates the premieres of five classical pieces that would later become masterworks. You'll be wishing you were there. (Kelly is also the author of a second, related book: *First Nights at the Opera*: Yale University Press, 2006.)

A History of Opera, Carolyn Abbate and Roger Parker: Norton, 2012
Much more than a basic chronology, this beautifully written single volume elaborates on the creation and reception of opera.

Listen, Joseph Kerman and Gary Tomlinson: 7th edition, Bedford/St Martin's, 2011
Worth checking out if you're interested in music's stylistic development across the centuries. Accompanying musical examples are on compact disc.

Listening in Paris: A Cultural History, James Johnson: University of California Press, 1995
It won't tell you how to listen but it will tell you how people did, past tense. Focusing on audiences in nineteenth-century Paris, Johnson offers a spectator's-eye

view of concert life and opera-going, explaining how and
why music listening became a sober and reverent affair.

Mozart's Grace, Scott Burnham: Princeton University
Press, 2012
Tries to get to the bottom of our perennial attraction to
Mozart's music, its characteristic beauty and loveliness.

On Mozart, James M. Morris, ed.: Cambridge University
Press, 1994
This book challenges some of the most ingrained
assumptions about Mozart, his working methods and
professional career.

Musicking: The Meanings of Performing and Listening,
Christopher Small: Wesleyan University Press, 1998
Music is not a thing but an activity – at least according
to Small. An impressive book that examines the social
relationships involved in making and hearing music.

Musicophilia: Tales of Music and the Brain, Oliver Sacks:
Vintage, 2008
Full of weird and wonderful stories about music's power
over the human brain. It's brainy stuff, blending insights
about music with scientific research.

*Real Men Don't Rehearse: Adventures in the Secret World of
Professional Orchestras*, Justin Locke: Justin Locke
Productions, 2005
A former double-bass player with the Boston Symphony
Orchestra, Locke exposes the lives of orchestral musicians,
both onstage and off.

Repeating Ourselves: American Minimal Music as Cultural Practice, Robert Fink: University of California Press, 2005
Argues for the existence of a post-Second World War 'culture of repetition' that links minimalist music to disco, Muzak, the craze for Vivaldi, and the infamous Suzuki teaching method.

The Rest is Noise: Listening to the Twentieth Century, Alex Ross: Picador, 2008
Topping many best-seller lists, this is the ultimate guide to modern classical music. You may also like Ross's *Listen to This* (Picador, 2011), an anthology of his articles for *The New Yorker*.

Stravinsky Inside Out, Charles Joseph: Yale University Press, 2001
A strikingly human portrait of the Russian composer, his professional relationships and public persona.

Why Classical Music Still Matters, Lawrence Kramer: University of California Press, 2009
A fresh take on the hoary question of whether classical music has any value and function in today's world.

Why Mahler? How One Man and Ten Symphonies Changed Our World, Norman Lebrecht: Anchor, 2011
A highly readable guide to Mahler's life and the enduring messages within his music.

As for recordings, here are my picks – some old, some new – of the works mentioned in this book:

The Barber of Seville, Rossini, conducted by Vittorio Gui, performed by the Royal Philharmonic Orchestra: EMI, 1963. Re-released 2002

Boris Godunov (1869 version), Mussorsgky, conducted by Valery Gergiev, performed by the Kirov Orchestra with Nikolai Putilin in the title role: Philips, 1999

Carmen, Bizet, conducted by Claudio Abbado, performed by the London Symphony Orchestra with Teresa Berganza as Carmen: Deutsche Grammophon, 1977. Re-released 2005

Concertos for Flute, Nos. 1 and 2, Mozart, conducted by Patrick Gallois, performed by the Swedish Chamber Orchestra with Gallois as soloist: Naxos, 2003

Cantatas, Bach, conducted by Sir John Eliot Gardiner, performed by the English Baroque Soloists and Monteverdi Choir: Soli Deo Gloria, 2005–8

Doctor Atomic, Adams, conducted by Lawrence Renes, performed by the Netherlands Philharmonic Orchestra with Gerald Finley in the title role: Opus Arte, 2008 (DVD)

Drysdale Overture, Lilburn, conducted by James Judd, performed by the New Zealand Symphony Orchestra: Naxos, 2006

Firebird, Stravinsky, conducted by Claudio Abbado, performed by the London Symphony Orchestra: Deutsche Grammophon, 1975. Re-released 1997

The Four Seasons, Vivaldi: conducted by Salvatore Accardo, performed by the Camera Italiana with Accardo as soloist: RCA, 1968. Re-released 1990

Hooked on Classics, conducted by Louis Clark, performed by the Royal Philharmonic Orchestra: Hooked on Classics, 1981. Re-released 2000

Missa Prolationum, Ockeghem, conducted by Edward Wickham, performed by The Clerks' Group: ASV, 1995

Mozart's Blue Dreams and Other Cross-Over Fantasies, performed by Joe Burgstaller and Hector Martignon: Summit, 2009

The Rite of Spring, Stravinsky, conducted by Herbert von Karajan, performed by the Berlin Philharmonic: Deutsche Grammophon, 1964. Re-released 2008

Samson, Handel, conducted by Raymond Leppard, performed by the English Chamber Orchestra with Robert Tear in the title role: Erato, 1980. Re-released 1993

Songs of a Wayfarer, Mahler, conducted by Michael Tilson Thomas, performed by the San Francisco Symphony with soloist Thomas Hampson: Sony BMG, 2010

Symphony No. 3, Lilburn, conducted by James Judd, performed by the New Zealand Symphony Orchestra: Naxos, 2002

Symphony No. 31 ('Paris'), Mozart, conducted by Sir Neville Mariner, performed by the Academy of St Martin in the Fields: Philips, 1990

Thirty-Nine Pages, Whitty, performed by Darragh Morgan (violin) and Mary Dullea (piano): Metier, 2009

Three Compositions for Piano, Babbitt, performed by Robert Taub: Harmonia Mundi, 1986

Wired: Works for Harpsichord and Electronics, performed by Jane Chapman: NMC, 2009

Glossary of technical terms

absolute music Music with no accompanying words and no dramatic or pictorial associations.

aria Solo song in opera, typically lyrical and expressive. An aria will not normally advance the plot but offer insight into a character's thoughts and feelings.

articulation Manner in which musical notes are accented, separated or joined together; articulation refers to the bowing of string players, tonguing of wind players, and finger-work of keyboardists.

atonality Absence of **key**; atonal music is based not on major or minor **scales** but on the entire spectrum of musical notes (all the black and white keys on the piano).

avant-garde Literally, advance guard. The term describes music that is innovative and experimental, pushing the boundaries of conventional style and structure.

bar Fixed unit of time comprising a given number of **beats**.

bar-line Vertical line drawn through musical **staff** (five parallel horizontal lines) to indicate the division of music into bars.

beat Music's background pulse, steady and constant.

canon Form of musical imitation in which one part is echoed and overlapped by another. Also referred to as **round**.

chord Cluster of notes (usually three or more) played simultaneously.

chromatic Notes that fall outside a given **key**.

consonance Combination of notes (usually two or more) that sounds stable and settled.

dissonance Combination of notes (usually two or more) that sounds tense and in need of resolution.

dynamics Music's volume, usually described in Italian terms: *forte* is loud, *piano* is quiet.

harmony Music's vertical sense – that is, the notes played simultaneously, usually structured as **chords**.

improvisation Spontaneous performance of music, without preparation or score-reading.

interval Distance in **pitch** between one note and another.

key Music based on a major or minor scale is said to be in a key; keys are identified by their first scale degree, called the **tonic** – for example, the key of C Major, B♭ Major, F Minor.

melody Succession of notes in a distinct form or shape.

metre Quantity and duration of **beats** in a **bar**, usually expressed in numerical form as a **time signature**; $\frac{3}{4}$, for example, means three beats per bar, each beat corresponding to the **note-value** of a crotchet.

mode Ancient musical scale that predates the major and minor scales used today. Much non-Western music is also based on modes.

note-value Length or duration of a note. Common note-values include crotchet, quaver (the value of which is half a crotchet) and minim (worth two crotchets).

octave **Interval** between two notes of the same (letter) name.

pedal Musical drone, most often played or sung by lowest instrument or bass voice.

pitch The technical term for a musical note, pitch refers to the frequency of a sound wave. This frequency needs to be stable and clear if a note is to be distinguished from mere noise.

phrase Musical sentence.

polyphony Type of musical **texture** featuring many voices or instrumental parts.

recitative Manner of singing approaching speech; used in opera to dramatic effect.

register Relative 'height' of a note or melody, height being an effect of **pitch**.

rhythm Manner in which notes of different durations are grouped together.

round *See* **canon**.

scale Eight consecutive notes arranged in ascending or descending order, where the first and eighth notes share the same (letter) name, and so span an **octave**. Classical music tends to use only two types of scale, major and minor, differentiated by the intervals between each of the eight notes.

score Music's notated form.

semitone Interval between a note and its closest neighbour (whether a black or white key on the piano). Two semitones make up the interval of a **tone**.

staff Horizontal axis of notated music; comprises five parallel lines.

tempo Speed, traditionally described in Italian terms: *allegro* for fast, *lento* for slow.

texture Manner in which instrumental parts or voices are woven together. Examples include **polyphony** and **canon**.

timbre Sonorous quality that differentiates one instrument from another.

time signature Numerical sign (notated at the start of a piece) designating musical **metre**.

tonality An organisational principle for musical pitch based on major and minor **scales**; tonal music can be said to be in a particular **key**.

tone Interval comprising two semitones.

tonic First degree of a musical **scale** and that which names a **key**; for example, the tonic of D Major is D.

ACKNOWLEDGEMENTS

Writing this book has proved to be a remarkably social and lively process, despite the solitary hours spent tapping away at the computer. Robert Constable and Allan Badley – former and current heads respectively of the School of Music, University of Auckland – have been a precious source of energy and ideas, taking the time to read and respond to earlier drafts. My students – especially those taking my course 'Contemporary Musical Culture' – have also helped shape my thinking, sometimes without even knowing it. At Awa Press, Mary Varnham has offered continual support and encouragement, not to mention careful and considered comments on the manuscript as it took shape. And my family and friends have continued to revitalise my interest in the project. Chris Bradley, in particular, deserves thanks for his companionship, kindness and gentle exuberance; his influence has been the greatest of gifts.

THE GINGER SERIES

Captivating Reads for Curious People

If you enjoyed this book, you may also like these from the award-winning series – available in both print and ebook editions.

How to Watch a Game of Rugby
Spiro Zavos

'One for all rugby lovers …
Spiro Zavos's best book yet'
Bryce Courtenay

Celebrated rugby writer Spiro Zavos shares his passion for the perfect game, and tackles some of the great mysteries: Did the Greeks invent rugby? Should players have pre-match sex? Which US president played fullback at Yale? An eye-opener for both rugby fans and those who don't know a ruck from a maul – yet.

How to Gaze at the Southern Stars
Richard Hall

'Will beguile experienced star-spotters and
absolute beginners alike'
New Scientist

Come on a tour of the heavens with astronomer extraordinaire Richard Hall. In this popular book, the founder of the acclaimed science centre Stonehenge Aotearoa weaves state-of-the-art science with the stories and myths of peoples across the globe and through the centuries. The night sky will never look the same again.

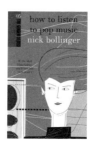

How to Catch a Fish
Kevin Ireland

'A small masterpiece'
The Dominion Post

Passionate angler Kevin Ireland has hunted on wild Irish lakes, clambered around ponds in medieval English abbeys, studied ancient texts, talked fishing with numerous other devotees, and spent thousands of hours actually with rod in hand. This charming book will delight everyone who follows the call of the wild.

How to Look at a Painting
Justin Paton

Winner
Montana Book Award for Contemporary Culture

Best Art Book of the Year
Listener, The Press, The Dominion Post

Major 12-part television series

In this brilliant book, acclaimed art writer Justin Paton takes us on a journey of exploration through the centuries and across the painted world – from the luscious fruit of Italy's Caravaggio to the lonely landscapes of New Zealand's Rita Angus, the dazzling panoramas of America's Lari Pittman and the mysterious 'tombstones' of Japan's On Kawara.

How to Catch a Cricket Match
Harry Ricketts

'Like the game itself, Ricketts casts an
enchanting spell'
The New Zealand Herald

Rudyard Kipling called cricketers 'flannelled fools'. Halfway through a
match, Groucho Marx asked when it would begin. Alfred Hitchcock used
cricketers as comic relief. Yet despite its notoriously slow pace, strange
language, eccentric umpires and frequent scandals, cricket is one of the
world's most loved sports. Read this book and find out why.

How to Watch a Bird
Steve Braunias

'A small and perfectly formed jewel'
The Sunday Star-Times

As prize-winning journalist Steve Braunias stands on an apartment
balcony on a sultry summer evening a black-backed gull flies so close he
is instantaneously bowled over with happiness. 'I thought: Birds,
everywhere. I wanted to know more about them.' This book is the result
– a moving personal journey into an amazing world.

How to Play a Video Game
Pippin Barr

'Conveys the joy and sense of
discovery in playing video games'
The Sunday Star-Times

Video games attract devotees of all ages and make more money than the movie industry, yet to many people they remain a mystery. Passionate game player and designer Pippin Barr shares fascinating insights that may entice you to give some games a whirl and provides some tips to take existing players to the next level.

How to Sail a Boat
Matt Vance

'A store of entertaining yarns'
New Zealand Listener

Matt Vance takes you inside the mind of a sailor, from the first scary moment of handling a boat solo to the exhilaration of sailing across oceans and discovering new worlds. His stories and those of his fellow madmen will captivate sailors young and old – and landlubbers may find themselves yearning for the blue horizon.

AWA PRESS

AWARD-WINNING PUBLISHERS OF INTELLIGENT
THOUGHT-PROVOKING NON-FICTION

See our authors talking about their books.

Find author events, special deals and competitions.

Stay up-to-date with our latest news.

Where to buy Awa Press books
PRINT EDITIONS: All good bookstores and at **awapress.com**
EBOOK EDITIONS: All major online etailers, including
Amazon, Kobo, Nook and iBooks.

Sign up for our newsletter at
awapress.com